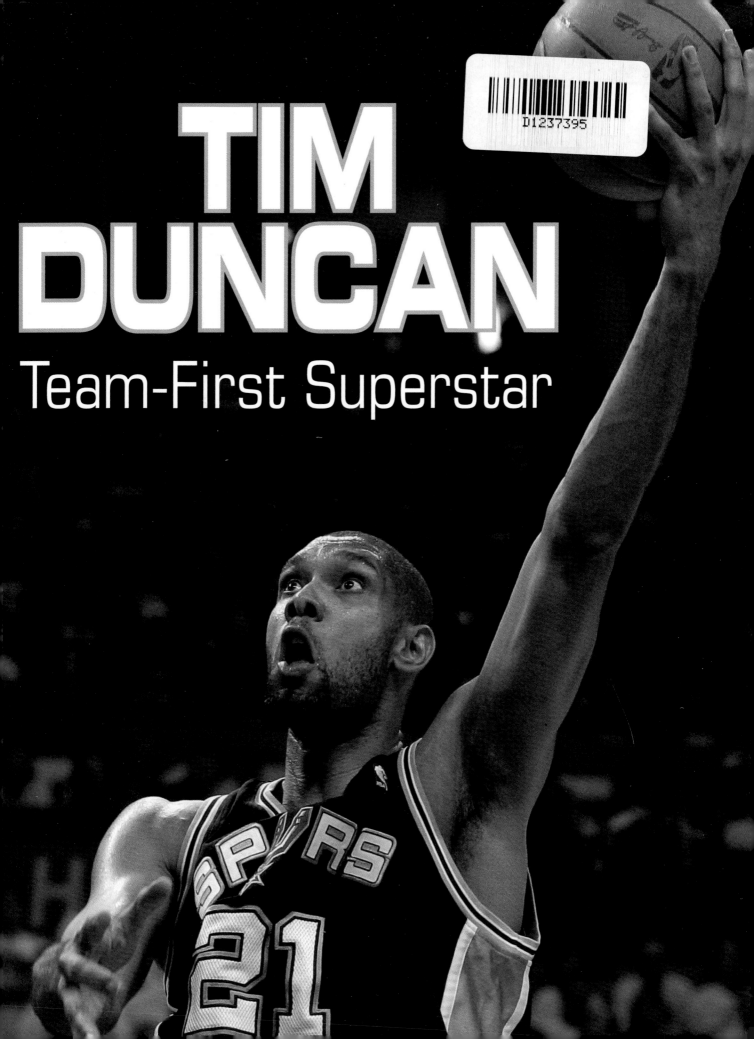

TIM DUNCAN
Team-First Superstar

Printed in U.S.A.
ISBN: 978-1-62937-407-9

Interior Design: Patricia Frey
Cover Design: Andy Hansen

Photos courtesy of AP Images
Cover photos by AP Images

CONTENTS

INTRODUCTION

By J.R. Wilco

Tim Duncan was a Spur for 19 years, and my favorite story about him takes place in a crowded locker room after a home game. The players are milling around, returning from the showers, getting dressed, and being interviewed. The Spurs routinely make two or three players available to the press after games, and it's usually one at a time and all of the media gather around each in turn. But on this night, there are several groups going at once: maybe Matt Bonner has a couple of writers asking him something, while Manu Ginobili is over there surrounded by about eight reporters, one with a video camera, and Danny Green is standing next to some radio guys, answering a question.

Tonight, instead of the usual orderly queue, it's a bit of a free-for-all when Duncan enters from the back. It's one of the nights that he's been made available to the media, and Tim is prepared to spend a few minutes with lights shining in his face, answering questions about the win or the loss—odds are it was a win. Only everybody's busy, and

no one has noticed that Duncan is politely standing at the edge of the room, ready to engage with the press.

A few moments go by as Duncan looks around, waiting patiently for any interested journalist to sidle over and ask him something. But no one does. Eventually he realizes that the room is collectively ignoring him; he isn't needed, and a smile spreads across his face as he does a low amplitude fist pump, turns on his heel, and exits the room. Press availability ended.

I love this story because of what it says about Tim. He never cared for the trappings, he was always about the substance. He was more comfortable bringing others into the limelight than he was standing in it. He was a family man with a job that sent him around the country, likely jealous of every minute taken from him that didn't directly touch basketball itself. If dealing with the media was a responsibility, he would fulfill it; if not, then he could get home that much sooner.

For someone who cares as much about family as Duncan, who spent so long in

Tim Duncan, alongside Tony Parker, cheers his teammates on from the bench during a 2012 overtime game against the Dallas Mavericks.

the same city with the same coach and teammates, privacy is almost second nature. What a perfect match, then, that he ended up with the San Antonio Spurs organization, where the wagons are perpetually circled. Here, questions are deferred with a simple "That's family business." If Gregg Popovich is the team's father figure, then Tim had to be the big brother. And what does an elder brother do but run interference for his siblings, show them all the tricks he's learned, and keep the group out of trouble?

It's that mindset that Duncan learned as he matured with the Spurs, and he put the team first no matter how brightly his star shone. He rejected the idea of the 21st century superstar as a global conglomerate, recognizing that if he could spend more time with his family instead of talking to the press, then he could spend more time with his team instead of building his brand. The stories of Tim's work ethic and leadership are many: how he was the first in the gym and the last to leave, how he would put up his own equipment after practice, how Brent Barry decided to join the Spurs after seeing Tim alone in the gym, working himself out during the summer.

As the seasons passed, Duncan made it a point to never leave the court at halftime or after a game until all of his teammates had left it. Whether they were being interviewed, saying goodbye to ex-teammates, or just taking their time, there would be Tim waiting under the basket to usher the last straggler back to the locker room.

Duncan took care of the team in the same way he had been taken care of. After injuring his left knee in his third year in the league, Popovich shut Tim down, refusing to let him jeopardize his longevity in the pursuit of a single season. That long view became the way the Spurs operated in both big things and small. As a result, Duncan became the first NBA superstar to be regularly held out of games. At first the reasons listed were the everyday gripes of the athlete—sore back or tight hamstring—but eventually the organization became more straightforward, listing the reason he Did Not Dress as: DND-OLD.

Tim Duncan shoots against Oklahoma City Thunder forward Nick Collison during a 2013 game.

A tireless mentor, Duncan helped groom Kawhi Leonard to be the next in a long line of Spurs superstars that started with George Gervin and David Robinson.

When rest alone wasn't enough, Duncan changed his eating habits and workout regimen to drop 20 pounds and save his knees the wear of the extra weight. I'll never forget the first time I saw Tim's new frame. I was in the AT&T Center on media row—above the 100s but just below the Baseline Bums—before a preseason game, and I didn't recognize him. He was wearing warmups, and I remember thinking, "Who's the long-limbed rookie bouncing around in the layup line?" Oh, just Tim Duncan. Looking as light on his feet and full of energy as he had 10 years earlier.

The way he looked after himself and his team, the relationships he developed with everyone from Pop, to Manu and Tony, to the 15th guy on the roster—this is what set him apart from your average basketball legend. These are the things that endeared him to so many fans. Tim was goofy, determined and genuine. He still is all of those things. He just doesn't play NBA basketball anymore.

But he'll always be a Spur. ★

THE LEGEND BEGINS

Duncan Arrived at Wake Forest Unheralded, Left a Star

By Bruno Passos

Tim Duncan discovered basketball on the island of St. Croix. He left his biggest mark on the game while in San Antonio with the Spurs. But between those two stops, over four years at Wake Forest University, Duncan made some of his greatest strides as a player, rising from promising freshman to one of the most decorated players the college game had ever seen. It's here that he made excellence a habit.

As a former swimming star with little competitive basketball under his belt by the age of 16, Duncan received interest from just four colleges, including Providence, Hartford, and Delaware State. He also met Wake Forest's coach Dave Odom, who made a trip to St. Croix on the chance recommendation of a former player and recent NBA draft pick, Chris King. While chatting one day, King mentioned to Odom he'd been impressed by a young player he'd seen while conducting basketball clinics in the Virgin Islands with Hornets center Alonzo Mourning. King didn't catch his name and couldn't recall which island he'd seen him on, but said that the kid "had a good game, and was the only player that stood up to Alonzo and me."

Odom eventually found and recruited him, and Duncan arrived at Wake Forest University in the fall of 1993, determined to fulfill the promise to get a college diploma he had made to his mother before she died of breast cancer. He joined a Demon Deacons team that already had junior point guard Randolph Childress (a future draft pick who would earn first-team All-ACC honors that

After an unmatched four-year career at Wake Forest, Duncan's jersey was retired following his final home game in Winston-Salem.

year) but played in a conference dominated by perennial powerhouses Duke and North Carolina.

Odom had expected to redshirt Duncan to allow him to develop his slight frame. But Duncan's performance upon arrival, paired with the unexpected ineligibility of the team's other big men recruits, opened the door for him to play immediately.

It's safe to say things worked out pretty well.

In his freshman season, Duncan averaged 9.8 points, 9.6 rebounds, and 3.8 blocks per game, showcasing his immaculate footwork and high basketball IQ. The Deacons finished third in the ACC, an improvement over the year before, but the future looked even brighter.

The Virgin Islander caught no one by surprise in his sophomore season. He was viewed as one of the country's top NBA prospects entering the year, and he lived up to the billing in every way. Assuming a larger role on the team, Duncan averaged 16.8 points, 12.5 rebounds, 4.2 blocks, and 2.1 assists per game, while winning National Defensive Player of the Year. Wake Forest finished first in the ACC and won the conference tournament, with Duncan and Childress earning first-team All-ACC honors and forming an imposing one-two combination.

No one would have held it against Duncan if he had left Wake Forest that summer for the NBA. Instead he stayed through his junior year and, when he was once again touted as the number-one overall pick the next summer, he decided to stay for his senior year. He was enjoying college, and would not yield to the pressure to cash in on his talent, adamant that we would keep his word to his mother.

Duncan led Wake Forest to two more great seasons—including another conference title—winning ACC Player of the Year twice, Defensive Player of the Year two

Tim Duncan and his dad, William, salute the Joel Coliseum crowd at the close of Duncan's Wake Forest career.

more times, and the Naismith, Rupp and Wooden awards in his senior year. The same unrelenting excellence that had become his calling card throughout his professional career took shape as he dominated opponents with his unique physical talents and his mastery of the fundamentals.

Meanwhile, Duncan's teammates had grown accustomed to his low-key demeanor and introverted nature. He made numerous connections during his Wake Forest days, but his relationship with senior walk-on Ken Herbst revealed Duncan's thoughtful nature. As Herbst said:

"He sensed my fear of flying and he gave me a shirt that was near and dear to his heart, and it was a 'No Fear' shirt… Tim always cut off the sleeves of his shirts. So it was more than a tank top, but a T-shirt without the sleeves. He gave me that shirt. I still have that shirt today."

Duncan graduated from Wake Forest as the winningest player in school history, leading the Deacons to a 97-31 record over his four-year career, but the fact that he graduated is what differentiates him from many other NBA superstars of his time. Kobe Bryant and Kevin Garnett both bypassed college during Duncan's career at Winston-Salem, and the prep-to-pros era was just gaining steam, with Dwight Howard, Amar'e Stoudemire and LeBron James all set to make the jump from high school.

He wasn't the only four-year college player to go number one in the draft (he wasn't even the last, that was Kenyon Martin in 2000), he never led his school beyond the Elite Eight, and he won't go down as the greatest player in NCAA

Named college basketball's most outstanding player in 1997, Duncan poses with the Wooden Award and the award's namesake, legendary UCLA coach, John R. Wooden.

history—although he's probably somewhere in the top 20. The lasting impression from his time at Wake Forest is that, despite how accomplished his college career was, his best still lay ahead of him. ★

MAKING HIS MARK

Duncan Shines Early and Often During His Rookie Season

By Michael Erler

It probably feels inevitable in retrospect that Tim Duncan, the top pick of the 1997 NBA draft and the unanimous winner of the Naismith College Player of the Year Award, the John R. Wooden Award, and the AP Player of the Year, would quickly develop into one of the consistently dominant players in league history. However, he wasn't convinced it would work out that way.

Even though he more than held his own in summer workouts with the legendary David Robinson, who had won the Most Valuable Player award just two seasons before, Duncan still had no pretensions about his place in the league and took the unusual step of volunteering to play in Summer League, something high lottery picks usually skipped at the time.

"I didn't know what to expect in the NBA," Duncan explained to teammate Manu Ginobili on the *Champions Revealed* interview that the Spurs participated in after winning the 2013-14 title. "I didn't know if I'd be good, or average, or bad or what it was. Right after I got drafted, Pop is like, 'There's Summer [League], do you want to go play?' and I was like, 'Hell, yeah I want to play. I want to get out there and get as much experience as possible.'"

What happened next has turned into one of the most oft-told anecdotes in Spurs lore. Duncan's first attempt of his professional career, a left-handed hook shot, was swatted into the stands by Utah's Greg Ostertag. As the story goes, Gregg Popovich had an immediate quip for his prized rookie, rolling his eyes and saying "Nice shot! ...

Duncan shakes hands with NBA Commissioner David Stern after being selected by the San Antonio Spurs as the first overall pick in the 1997 NBA Draft.

We're going to be real good this year," only for Duncan to come back right at his coach with "I told you you screwed up drafting me."

Looking back on it years later, Duncan didn't pull any punches on his debut. "I sucked!" he told Ginobili. "I was awful."

He's likely exaggerating for effect (Popovich went on to explain that Duncan blocked Ostertag's shot on the next trip down the floor) and it's telling that it was early in training camp that Popovich and his assistants made the significant decision to flip the roles of their two main big men. It'd be the kid receiving the lion's share of opportunities in the low post, leaving the veteran Robinson to be the "dive man" to clean up on offensive rebounds and through other secondary offensive opportunities from the high post.

To his everlasting credit, Robinson never uttered a peep of complaint over the change in status, and though he couldn't have known it at the time, he was setting an example to his protégé about how to act when the day came where he too would have to surrender offensive responsibility to younger players.

Duncan was as good as advertised almost from the beginning—"I have seen the future and he wears No. 21," none other than Charles Barkley declared after a preseason game against Houston—and he would indeed go on to capture the league's Rookie of the Month award in each month of the season, but he wasn't a 20-point, 10-rebound metronome, not at first.

After a solid 15-point, 10-rebound opening effort in a win at Denver, Duncan was held to a modest nine points and five boards in his home opener against Cleveland, forced to play just 23 minutes due to foul trouble. In fact, Duncan didn't crack 20 points until the seventh game of his career, at Minnesota against future rival Kevin Garnett. Through his first 21 games Duncan only eclipsed the 20-point barrier three times.

Duncan averaged 15.2 points through November, then 19.3 in December, and 19.5 in January. He'd already established himself as a double-double machine by then, racking up 10 of them in his first 20 games and then 15 more in the next 20. He had a season-high 22 rebounds in just his third game.

But it wasn't until February that his scoring really took off. He went on to average 25.7 points that month, 23.8 in March and then 26.9 down the stretch in April. Tentative and conscientious about moving the ball and getting his teammates involved at first, Duncan eventually got comfortable enough to regularly take 18-20 shots a night, and he was constantly expanding his repertoire on the low block, learning what worked against whom.

After losing to Barkley and the Rockets in their first regular season meeting, Duncan and the Spurs were much better in a win the second go-around, and he kept playing better against Shaquille O'Neal and the Lakers every time he faced them.

Mere numbers can't adequately explain Duncan's performances, of course. While he would go on to remain a valuable contributor

Duncan shows off his 1998 NBA Rookie of the Year trophy, which he won by unanimous vote.

to the very end, even as a 40-year-old, it's almost hard to remember what a fluid athlete he was early in his career. No, he was never as freakish in terms of foot speed or leaping ability as Robinson —Duncan's made self-disparaging comments about his lack of hops for years— but he could seriously move in his younger days and had the quickness and lateral agility to flummox just about any defender. He was the complete package, the ultimate combination of length, fundamentals and feel. That Duncan had Robinson to spar with every day in practice only hastened his development. He wasn't going to find a tougher defender in the league than the one in his own gym.

Duncan went on to win the league's Rookie of the Year award in a unanimous vote and was named First-Team All-NBA as well as Second-Team All-Defensive, both incredibly rare accolades for a first-year player. He led the Spurs to a first-round upset against the Suns, setting the tone with 32 points in the series opener, but absorbed some harsh lessons from Karl Malone in the Western semi-finals as the Spurs went down to the Jazz in five games. Just how quick a study Duncan was would become obvious in his second season. ★

Duncan laughs with reporters during a press conference in San Antonio, just months before the start of his sterling rookie campaign.

CHAMPS!

Duncan Powers Spurs to First NBA Title, Wins Series MVP

By Jesus Gomez

In a way it's fitting that Tim Duncan and the Spurs' first championship came under strange circumstances. The lockout-shortened season of 1999 was hard on everyone. Michael Jordan retired, leaving a power vacuum. Some of the league's best players showed up out of shape and teams saw big swings in performance. San Antonio started out 6-8 for the year, and coach Gregg Popovich was rumored to be on the hot seat—not exactly the type of performance expected of a championship contender.

In this unpredictable atmosphere, a team that could keep their cool and just play had an edge. Tim Duncan didn't need chaos to be at his best, but he wasn't hindered by it either, which is a key reason why the Spurs raised the banner.

It was a transitional year for the league. The Jazz were hoping to finally get to the "promised land" with Jordan out of the way, the Lakers were shuffling players around in an attempt to find a winning combination, and the Trail Blazers were still a year or two away from contending. The East was weak at the top but had parity. There were bound to be surprises, like an eighth seed reaching the Finals without its best player or an Isaiah Rider-led team taking out everyone's title favorite.

In that context, Duncan's almost metronomic performances stand out even more. He only had a few sub-par showings despite appearing in all 50 games and playing 39 minutes a night, including two instances where he had to play on three consecutive nights, a scheduling necessity

In just his second season, Tim Duncan led the Spurs to an NBA Championship and was named NBA Finals MVP.

when a league has to squeeze what would normally be four months worth of games into three. Duncan's averages of 22 points, 11 rebounds, two assists and two blocks made him a lock for both First Team All-NBA honors and a First All-Defensive team selection. He finished third in MVP voting behind Karl Malone and Alonzo Mourning despite sharing the court with another star that played essentially the same position.

Duncan paced a Spurs team that lacked the offensive firepower to survive bad games from its stars, so they built their identity around a defense that featured two all-time big men defenders. David Robinson was still a force in his own right, but his decline on offense was starting to be noticeable. The Spurs were Duncan's team and they were going to need their sophomore star to perform at his best even more consistently than the most grizzled veterans, under unique circumstances that were throwing off others far more accomplished.

After nabbing the first seed in the Western Conference thanks to owning a tiebreaker over the Jazz, the Spurs faced Kevin Garnett's Timberwolves. Garnett's record-breaking contract was considered to be one of the reasons the lockout happened in the first place but he was worth every penny of the six-year, $126 million deal he signed. Even through the turmoil of the Stephon Marbury trade, Minnesota was dangerous, but the Spurs eliminated them in four games. San Antonio was on a mission.

Waiting for them in the second round were the Lakers. Shaquille O'Neal and Kobe Bryant were monsters, combining for 45 points a night. They still couldn't do anything to prevent a Spurs sweep powered by Duncan's 29 points, 11 rebounds, three assists, a steal and two blocks per game. While Robinson couldn't get going on offense, Sean Elliott and Jaren Jackson stepped up to fill the void. In two rounds, the Spurs had taken out two of the best big men in the West and everything pointed towards a power-forward showdown between Duncan and Malone.

Instead, the Blazers upset the Jazz, depriving us of a match-up for the ages and adding more randomness to a season that already had plenty. The series against the Blazers, which ended up being yet another sweep, did not completely lack in drama, providing an indelible moment in that championship run, which we now know as "The Memorial Day Miracle." Elliott shot his way into immortality in Game 2 by hitting a go-ahead three-pointer late in the game to cap a huge comeback before a delirious Alamodome crowd. Duncan, meanwhile, racked up 23 points, 10 rebounds and five blocks to make that moment possible. San Antonio cruised comfortably through the remaining two games when the series shifted to Portland.

Then the Finals came against a surprising Knicks team that clawed its way up from the eighth seed without their best player, Patrick Ewing. The Spurs were obviously expected to beat them, but New York had defied logic and exceeded expectations for three rounds. Allan Houston and Latrell Sprewell gave the

Duncan receives a pass while being guarded by New York Knicks forward Larry Johnson during Game 2 of the 1999 NBA Finals.

Knicks a huge edge in talent and athleticism at the wing and San Antonio had to counter with its size advantage inside.

With the Spurs leading the series 3-1, Game 5 in New York was a microcosm of the season: chaotic and wild with unexpected swings but ultimately dominated by the best young player in the league.

The Spurs couldn't buy a bucket early. The Knicks' defensive effort focused on the paint, severely limiting penetration and working to keep Duncan and Robinson from getting deep position. On offense, Houston and Sprewell destroyed Mario Elie and Elliott. The Knicks led for most of the first half, and were able to push their advantage up to eight points. Duncan kept San Antonio in the game by hitting the outside looks that New York allowed, while Robinson feasted on a raw Marcus Camby. Duncan and Robinson combined for 26 of the Spurs' 40 first-half points and after 24 minutes, the Spurs were somehow up two.

Though the Knicks played with increased urgency after halftime, their energy worked against them. They turned the ball over, allowing the Spurs to go on a run in the beginning of the third quarter. But then New York became extremely disruptive, turning to a full court press and gambling for steals, which prevented the Spurs from running their offense. Sprewell caught fire, the Knicks caught up to San Antonio and it seemed like they were going to run away with it, forcing a Game 6. Unfortunately for the Knicks, the Spurs still had Duncan.

From the end of the third quarter through the beginning of the fourth, Duncan scored 14 of the Spurs' 16 points. He answered every Sprewell basket with one of his own, and when Jeff Van Gundy started to double team him, he consistently made the right pass. All along, Duncan's fantastic defense was present. The Spurs closed out the series by executing in crunch time but Duncan was the one that made it all possible by saving them when they were at their worst.

Though he was rightfully awarded Finals Most Valuable Player, Duncan didn't do anything out of the ordinary. He simply played like he always did. When things were going well for the Spurs, his performance looked workmanlike and mechanical. When they weren't, that perception changed. All of a sudden, hitting a banker and contesting a shot can seem downright heroic.

In 1999, one of the weirdest, most unpredictable seasons in modern NBA history, the stoic, unflinching persona that Duncan forged at Wake Forest helped him scale the NBA's mountaintop. He faced chaos and uncertainty unfazed. The edge he earned by keeping his cool became the trademark he would be known for through the rest of his career, along with his bank-shot and his tip-toe blocks. ★

As the final buzzer sounds to end Game 5 against the New York Knicks, Duncan celebrates his first NBA championship with the Spurs.

BACK ON TOP

Spurs and Duncan Further Validated with Second Championship

By D.P. Jones

Tim Duncan and the Spurs are NBA Champions once again.

After four long years, the Larry O'Brien trophy returns to South Texas, and with that return comes an undeniable sense of validation. With the Spurs not even so much as sniffing the Finals since their celebration on the floor of Madison Square Garden in 1999, fans could be forgiven for wondering if the likes of Kobe, Shaq, and Phil were destined to forever relegate their team to bridesmaid status.

Things were supposed to be different after that first championship. Tim Duncan signed a long-term contract that would keep him in San Antonio through his prime, David Robinson's back had held up, and young Tony Parker hit the ground running on his NBA career, dicing up opponents with his jitterbug moves. Yet for all the team had done right, there seemed to be no getting past their nemesis out West.

As Los Angeles extended their string of championships, critics came out of the woodwork, echoing Jackson's taunts about asterisks. Hadn't the Spurs' lone championship only come because the league was in disarray after the lockout? Who could say whether this version of the Spurs, a strange combination of veterans and fresh faces, could go all the way?

"There was some hope there," Robinson said at the beginning of the season, "but also some shakiness, a little disappointment because we didn't think we were consistent enough." Where past Spurs teams had struggled to find the confidence to execute in big games, this year's team took on the

Tim Duncan poses with teammate and mentor David Robinson after powering the Spurs to another NBA championship in 2003, Robinson's final season. The two players shared *Sports Illustrated*'s 2003 Sportsmen of the Year award.

unshakable determination of its leader. Duncan simply refused to let his team fail.

Against Jason Kidd and the New Jersey Nets in the deciding Game 6 of The Finals, the reigning two-time MVP put on such a display of dominance that to describe it with statistics seems ridiculously reductive. If you like that sort of thing, I suppose there is Tim's newly-minted NBA record for blocks in a seven game series. But a greater demonstration by far is the steady hand Duncan demonstrated both throughout the Finals and the Spurs' playoff run, pushing his team to keep going and patting them on the butt when they made big plays, things seventh year Coach Gregg Popovich calls "Larry Bird stuff."

The Spurs were challenged in each round by Phoenix, L.A., Dallas, and New Jersey, but capitalized each time they had a chance to eliminate their opponent away from the SBC Center. Over the playoffs, they went 3-0 in road elimination games. True, a 16-8 playoff record places these Spurs somewhere below the '99 team (15-3) in the rankings for greatest championship runs, but this title was about more than how many games it took.

As arguably the top big man in the game today, Duncan needed no validation. But his team did, especially after Lakers coach Phil Jackson declared their first championship an aberration and then backed up his talk by twice eliminating San Antonio in dominating fashion. The fans in the Alamo City may scoff at the notion but the 2003 Spurs, who still featured three players from that 1999 team in Duncan, Robinson, and Malik Rose, needed

to remove that asterisk. In defeating Jackson's Lakers in the Western Conference Semifinals and shattering the Shaq-Kobe dynasty, they got 90 percent of the way there. To complete the journey, they had to fight the inevitable lull which sabotaged them at home in Game 1 against Dallas and Game 2 against New Jersey. Each time they stumbled, Duncan was there to keep them going.

Some might remark that no team which features Stephen Jackson as its second most consistently dynamic player—or which benches its starting point guard in favor of Speedy Claxton—should have gotten anywhere near an NBA Finals. This is a team which ended the 2002 calendar year with a 19-13 record and sported a pedestrian point differential. It was a squad featuring 1990s retreads Steve Smith, Danny Ferry, and Steve Kerr. Even in the playoffs, these Spurs gave their fans panic attacks with multiple blown double-digit leads. To history, this may not cut the figure of a championship team, but Robinson will remember it differently. "Our team is a throwback mix of character and determination. We just do things the right way."

So let history note that a team which employed a 37-year-old Robinson and a 40-year-old Kevin Willis as contributing members of its frontcourt took down Amar'e Stoudemire, Shaq, Dirk, and Kenyon Martin. Let it show that they tore through the 2003 portion of the calendar at a 41-9 pace. Most crucially, this was a team which featured a player who may end up among the greatest of his generation.

Duncan reaches to get a hand on the ball as the New Jersey Nets' Dikembe Mutombo drives to the basket in Game 4 of the NBA Finals.

"Having Tim here was like a gift from God," Robinson said.

Clichés rarely get updated, but that old saw about horseshoes and hand grenades deserves an amendment after Duncan's 46-minute, 21-20-10-8 opus in Game 6. From now on, near-quadruple doubles in clinching NBA Finals games are added to the list of near-misses that garner full accreditation. This is the new shorthand for dominant playoff performances. We'll call it Duncan's "near-quadruple double game."

For the series, Timmy averaged 24.2 points, 17 rebounds, 5.3 assists, and 5.3 blocks. Compare it to Shaq's 36-12-4-2 against the Nets the year before and it speaks to the breadth of Duncan's game. There is literally nothing he cannot do. Okay, so he can't pop three-pointers like Dirk. But you get the sense he can make him when he has to. And yeah, Tim is sometimes shaky from the free throw line. But his 71% rate this season is Rick Barry-esque compared to Shaq's 62 percent.

Duncan pops celebratory champagne with teammates Steve Smith and Kevin Willis after the Spurs beat the New Jersey Nets in six games to win the NBA Championship.

He's the most complete player since pre-Wizards Jordan. He saved the Spurs franchise in San Antonio when he spurned the advances of Doc Rivers and the Orlando Magic, and he saved them in the history books this year. By defeating New Jersey, Duncan and the Spurs have avoided one-hit wonder status. This team is not doomed to be dismissed like Wes Unseld's Washington Bullets or Barry's Golden State Warriors.

But neither is it a dynasty. Not yet. With Robinson's departure, the transition is finally complete. Just as The Admiral never won a ring before Duncan arrived, there will be questions about whether Duncan can repeat without his mentor and fellow "Twin Tower." The championship image of Robinson holding aloft the Larry O'Brien trophy and Duncan beside him with the Finals MVP trophy echoed 1999. It also underscored Spurs' fans anxiety that Robinson's departure might mean the loss of the team's character. Robinson is so integral to what the Spurs are, he's still the last player to be introduced before games. Rose called him "The heart and soul of the team."

But as a validating title run gives way to a summer of uncertainty, the Spurs know they can lean on Duncan. Tim has proved that he can carry a team to a championship as its lone superstar. He's the type of player the Spurs have never had before, and he's taken them places they've never been. The Spurs have lost an Admiral, but with Duncan in command, this is a team poised to remain a championship contender for years to come. ★

After tearing his way through the 2003 season, Duncan was named both NBA MVP and NBA Finals MVP.

THRICE IS NICE

Duncan Overcomes Struggles to Help Spurs Claim Third Crown

By Kyle Carpenter

The entire 2004-05 season came down to a quarter. The 82 game regular season and 22 playoff contests that led to this point weren't exactly irrelevant, but they were sitting in a box marked "NARRATIVE: open only in case of victory." It was the last twelve minutes of the first NBA Finals Game 7 in over a decade.

The Pistons, maybe the most resilient team in history, withstood a potentially insurmountable 2-0 deficit, bounced back after Robert Horry's Game 5, didn't flinch as Manu Ginobili devised every possible Pythagorean angle to get a human body from the three-point line to the rim, and met the challenge of a vintage performance from Tim Duncan, who had recently been described by Mike D'Antoni, the coach of reigning MVP Steve Nash, as "the ultimate winner... the best player in the game."

As the confetti is being swept up and a Riverboat parade is in the works; with a third championship secured and the cornerstones of a legacy in place, it's fair to look back and see how we got here. The march to the final quarter of this year's Finals began on May 13th of 2004 when San Antonio Spurs' title defense effectively ended after Tim Duncan's all-time great playoff shot was answered by Derek Fisher's unfathomable 0.4 second rebuttal.

After losing David Robinson, Steve Kerr, Danny Ferry, and Stephen Jackson (retirement, retirement, front office, and free agency, respectively), the Spurs faced an uphill battle to repeat. But the Spurs couldn't get past the Lakers, and the Detroit Pistons made Fisher's time-bending shot irrelevant. By handily defeating L.A. in the Finals, Detroit sowed the last seeds of dissent that

2005 saw the Spurs win their third NBA championship in eight years since drafting Tim Duncan.

broke up one of the game's all-time great tandems. Both Phil Jackson and Shaquille O'Neal left Los Angeles, which meant that the Pistons' convincing victory deprived the Spurs of a chance at retribution, as the Lakers sans-Shaq-and-Phil finished out of the playoffs in 2003.

Though the league's two most-recent champions each entered the postseason at the #2 seed, the top-seeded Heat and Suns were heavily favored. Phoenix possessed the league's best record, the MVP, Coach of the Year, GM of the Year and the third best win increase in NBA history. Along with them, the Dwyane Wade and Shaq-led Heat were the toast of the league, each playing an exciting brand of basketball. But ultimately the NBA Finals came down to the teams with the best defensive units.

The Spurs played smothering defense in the first two games and held the Pistons to 69 points in Game 1, their second lowest point total of the season. Duncan and Ginobili executed well on their home court to open the series with a 2-0 lead and an impressive 36-point differential. However, the Pistons countered with an even more remarkable 48-point differential over the first two games at the Palace with phenomenal team defense, and Ben Wallace's stellar individual effort.

In a crucial game 5—with the series now effectively a Best-of-Three—the Spurs were 60 seconds away from taking a commanding 3-2 lead on the Piston's own home court. With an 88-87 lead and Duncan at the free throw line for two, it seemed like the Spurs were lining themselves up for a sure thing.

But then, the unthinkable. Having already missed his first three free throw attempts of the quarter, Duncan stood at the line and missed both.

When he returned to the line with the chance to give the Spurs the lead with 34 seconds left, Duncan missed another crucial free throw to mark six consecutive missed shots. He made the second to tie the game, but then proceed to miss a completely open put-back with a second remaining.

A game that the Spurs could have won handily was forced into overtime.

Had it not been for Robert Horry's heroic night (scoring 21 points in the 4th quarter and overtime, the first time he had scored more than 18 points since he arrived in San Antonio) and especially the "Big Shot Bob" 3-pointer with 5.8 seconds to steal the win from Detroit, the Pistons would have won Game 5 and probably the 2005 NBA Championship.

Duncan called his performance "an absolute nightmare," which is an incredible way to describe a 26-point, 19-rebound outing.

He recovered to play well, if unspectacular by his lofty standards, in Game 6. But the Spurs didn't quite have enough to close out the series against a Pistons team who added poise to the cornered-animal-fighting-to-survive intensity that only a champion can muster.

As a testament to how closely matched the teams were, neither the Spurs nor the Pistons led by double digits in any of the last three games of the NBA Finals. They

Duncan battles with Detroit Pistons' Antonio McDyess during the fourth quarter of Game 7 in 2005.

were trading powerful, measured punches in a beautiful brawl. Of course these two teams who mirrored each other in so many ways would find themselves in a 24-quarter stalemate.

Tim Duncan had to battle not only the stifling frontcourt of the Pistons, but his own, rarely-seen mortality. "It was about just kind of pushing through it and just the perseverance," Duncan said. "My teammates

A second-half burst from the Spurs was enough to overpower the Pistons in a hard-fought and low-scoring Game 7 win.

just continued to throw the ball to me. They were more confident in me than I was."

This wasn't quite the 37-point, 16-rebound master class Duncan gave the Lakers two years ago in derailing L.A.'s three-peat, but Duncan showed his teammates' confidence to be well-founded.

With the Pistons front court in foul trouble, Duncan scored 12 of his 25 points in the third quarter (including 4-for-4 from the line), taking over the game and leading the Spurs out of a nine-point hole.

A Game 7, where you don't win so much as you outlast your opponent, was starting the fourth quarter all square. Like a heavyweight prizefight heading into the 15th round even on the scorecard, the Spurs and Pistons found themselves 12 minutes from a decision.

With Duncan clearly asserting himself, Pistons coach Larry Brown began calling for double-teams, a strategy that the Pistons had avoided for most of the series. This inside-out play opened up the space for the game-breaking triples that came from Horry, Bruce Bowen, and Manu Ginobili in the final period. Manu seemed particularly liberated and scored 11 of his 23 in the 4th quarter, including the crucial final free throws to put the game out of reach.

It wasn't easy. It wasn't glorious. But it was finished.

"It was such a long, tough year for us," Duncan said. "But all the guys fought so hard."

And because of that indefatigable fight, the San Antonio Spurs are your 2005 NBA Champions. Let there be honking and talk of a dynasty and discussion of superlatives, legacies, and placement in all-time rankings. The basketball is done and it is time for the good stuff. It's time for the narrative. ★

Along with winning his third NBA championship, Tim Duncan was awarded his third NBA Finals MVP award.

DYNASTY

Spurs Sweep Cavs to Capture Fourth Title

By Chris Itz

The Spurs were bounced out of the 2006 playoffs by the Dallas Mavericks in one of the greatest series in NBA history, an epic seven-game, second-round match-up that solidified what is perhaps the best current rivalry in the league. That heartbreaking defeat—the Spurs were just one misguided Manu Ginobili foul on Dirk Nowitzki away from completing not just a 3-1 series comeback but a 20-point Game 7 comeback as well—unquestionably served as competitive fuel for the team to get back to the top.

In the 2007 playoffs, the Spurs went 16-5 but endured a few tests along the way. They lost the opening playoff game to the Denver Nuggets before rattling off four straight wins, and there were the Phoenix Suns in the second round. As the Suns were evening the series at two apiece, San Antonio caught a break when Robert Horry hip-checked

Steve Nash into the scorers table at the end of Game 4, which resulted in one-game suspensions for Amar'e Stoudemire and Boris Diaw after they stepped onto the court to come to Nash's defense.

The Spurs went on to win a tight Game 5 in Phoenix and closed it out at home in Game 6. Every championship run needs a little luck along the way and San Antonio capitalized on the situation. The Spurs were further helped by a huge first-round upset that saw the 67-win, first-seeded Mavericks lose in six games to Stephen Jackson, Baron Davis, and the rest of Don Nelson's upstart Golden State Warriors. Instead of the Mavericks waiting for the Silver and Black in the Western Conference Finals it was Deron Williams and the Utah Jazz, who the Spurs took care of in a mere five games.

This Finals pairing was never really supposed to be much of a series, and the

Tim Duncan soars above Drew Gooden of the Cleveland Cavaliers in Game 3 of the 2007 NBA Finals.

After a crushing Game 7 loss to the Dallas Mavericks in the 2006 Western Conference Semifinals, the Spurs rebounded in 2007 with a four-game rout of the Cleveland Cavaliers to reclaim the NBA championship.

San Antonio Spurs finished their sweep of the Cleveland Cavaliers. The Game 4 win brought the South Texas franchise their fourth championship, all coming in the last nine seasons with Gregg Popovich at the helm and Tim Duncan as the team's quiet leader and superstar. San Antonio entered the series as overwhelming 1-5 favorites, odds which implied an 83.3 percent chance of San Antonio being the last team standing. Put another way, losing in four to the Spurs was not an indictment of 22-year-old LeBron James or the Cavaliers, it was a likely outcome. The Cavaliers were simply over-matched at almost every position on the court.

The two games in Cleveland were fairly close affairs, a welcome change of pace after the two dominating wins for the Spurs in San Antonio—the Spurs took a 15-point lead into the fourth quarter of Game 1 and a 25-point lead into the half of Game 2 behind excellent offensive play from Tony Parker.

Parker, who even the most casual of fans would have to describe as lightning quick in open space, was too much for Daniel "Boobie" Gibson to handle and the Frenchman shot a fiery 57 percent from the floor for the series, getting the lion's share of his points at the rim. Except for a slow start in Game 3, Parker was a one-man-fast-break machine, constantly showing off his acceleration and top speed on his way to one incredible finish after another, many ending in typical Parker fashion—with the point guard sliding across the hardwood out of bounds toward the cameramen and looking back to watch the ball drop through the net. TP was rewarded with his first NBA Finals MVP award for his brilliant effort, having scored 28 percent of San Antonio's points in the series and posting a 25-5-3 line in the Finals.

In typical Spurs fashion, San Antonio did the bulk of their damage on the defensive end of the floor, holding the Cavs to an average of 80.5 points per game on just 39 percent shooting from the floor and a frigid 29 percent from deep. The Cavaliers' 80.5 points per game is the second lowest scoring average in Finals history, just behind the 1999 New York Knicks. Not coincidentally,

Duncan and longtime teammate Tony Parker celebrate with the 2007 championship trophy and the Finals MVP trophy.

the Spurs won their first championship in that 1999 lockout-shortened season, beating the Knicks in five games and holding New York to just 79.8 points per contest.

The entire San Antonio team deserves credit for their stinginess in their own end, but special appreciation should be given to the incredible effort that 36-year old Bruce Bowen showed in guarding one of the game's best in LeBron James. The defensive ace led the Spurs in minutes played in the series, and despite not having a single play called for him on the offensive end, he gave everything he had in helping to limit LeBron to just 36 percent shooting. Bowen did have a nice offensive Game 3 when SA's Big Three struggled, shooting 4-5 from three, but his paycheck was earned on the other end. He won't get a ton of praise for his work, and guarding James is most certainly a team effort, but Bowen's work was absolutely vital in the Spurs winning their fourth championship.

Then there's Tim Duncan, who won his fourth title but didn't pick up what should probably have been his fourth Finals MVP award. The veteran big man was even more unsexy than usual on the offensive end, scoring just 18 points a game on 45 percent shooting (a little over six points less than Parker per game and considerably less efficient), and that probably swayed the voting media toward Parker and his great offensive performance in the series.

But the voters got it wrong, or at least there is a great argument that Tim should have gotten the nod. The Spurs won the series with defense and there's no question who is the center of everything for the Spurs on that end. Big Fun is the captain, the middle linebacker if you will, calling assignments out and directing traffic while also serving as the team's last line of defense. Timmy used his length and understanding of angles and position to make scoring at the rim a daunting prospect for the Cavaliers even when they beat their man on the perimeter. Duncan had the best defensive rating (91) on the team (97.2 for the team over the series) by a fairly wide margin.

Tim didn't lead the team in scoring, but he did lead the Spurs in rebounds, assists, steals and blocks for the series as well as setting the steady, calm-but-totally-focused tone that allowed the Spurs to endure Cavaliers rallies in Games 3 and 4 and pull out close wins.

Of course, Tim himself probably doesn't really care. When Tony Parker was presented with the Finals MVP, it was Duncan who was visibly the most happy for Parker. It's hard not to root for a guy whose selflessness and team-first ethos is so genuine.

With this championship the Spurs have established themselves as a dynasty, although a non-traditional one. The franchise's fourth title moves them into elite company where they join the Celtics, Lakers and Bulls as the only teams that have won at least four NBA championships. ★

Duncan and Fabricio Oberto are energized in the closing minutes of Game 4, knowing they've clinched the title for the Spurs.

THE EVOLVING GAME OF TIM DUNCAN

Duncan Adapts His Body and Game for Modern NBA

By Matthew Tynan | November 21, 2012

Don't say you saw it coming, because you didn't.

Over the summer of 2012, we wondered how much was left in the tank after he re-signed with the only team he's ever known, but Tim Duncan's supposed farewell tour has turned into a display of resurgence. And the gas gauge certainly seemed on the verge of empty when the Phoenix Suns swept the Spurs out of the playoffs in 2010. Steve Nash and Amar'e Stoudemire had pick-and-rolled the future Hall-of-Famer to death, taking advantage of his diminishing athleticism and decreasing foot speed on the way to a dominant performance over the team that had haunted Phoenix's playoff dreams for years.

But at 36 years of age, Duncan has reinvented himself, trashing the "old dog" idiom and redefining the list of tricks he was capable of being taught. The old 4-down, throw-it-in-the-post Duncan still makes his mark at times, but as the remnants of the throwback big man in the NBA fades, The Big Fundamental continues to incorporate new tweaks into an already legendary game.

Gregg Popovich sees it. After all, he's helped refine the system for which his big man is the cornerstone. As the Spurs have evolved from a batten-down-the-hatches, defense-oriented juggernaut to a high-speed pick-and-roll machine (though not to the same extent as last season), Pop has asked Duncan to play differently. The style of play

Showing he still has more in the tank, Tim Duncan leaves the Utah Jazz defenders in the dust during the 2012 playoffs.

that won four titles and two league MVPs was no longer feasible.

So the winningest coach-player combination in history continues to work toward that fifth title, and all along the way, opponents and media members alike can't help but ask Pop the same question: how? How is Tim Duncan doing this? The coach hears the question daily but doesn't seem to mind answering, filling recorders with related quotes that could go on for days.

Really, it's because he's just as amazed. And whether Pop's getting soft in his old age or Duncan's getting more ornery in his, the big man is getting to call his own shots.

"I've already tried to sit him in a couple of back-to-backs, and he has not allowed me to," Pop said prior a game against the Clippers. "I ask him, 'who do (you) think is running this program?' And then he tells me.

"I say 'OK.'"

But what Popovich has noticed, along with the rest of us, is the athleticism Duncan is playing with at his age. He's never been a leaper or a high-flyer; his fundamentals and foot speed took him a long way and continue to do so.

"He's reduced his weight the last three years and works all summer on flexibility … he's really disciplined about what he puts in his body," Pop continued. "He's got some explosiveness in his drives and he's expanded his game. Like Michael (Jordan) learned to shoot more instead of dunking everything."

And this is where Duncan has evolved most noticeably: he has become a more versatile shooter.

"Timmy's learned to knock down the jumpers on the elbows and on the wings,

because he's not going to go down in the post and amaze people every time anymore," Pop said. "So he picks and chooses."

While Duncan still has the ability to isolate, the incorporation of floating jumpers from elbow to elbow and shots coming off pin-down screens have made him as tricky a cover as ever. And the numbers prove it. Duncan isn't necessarily a child of the age of advanced statistics, but he has been grandfathered in.

If the season were to end today (I know, it's only eleven games in, but humor me), Duncan would have his highest true-shooting percentage in six years (56.4), his highest PER (27.4, good enough for second in the league behind LeBron James), defensive-rebounding percentage (30.5), steal percentage (1.7) and block percentage (6.7) of his career, as well as the lowest turnover percentage (7.9) he's ever had. He's been a monster on both sides of the floor, but his defense has been most impressive. Duncan is currently averaging more blocks per 36 minutes (3.2) than in any other season of his career.

While these stats might put things in perspective, you certainly don't need them to appreciate the level at which he's playing. As Pop said recently, the only stat he's truly concerned about is the number under the 'W' column. Yes, this is as Popovichian an answer as you'll see, one that won't be a featured topic of discussion at next year's Sloan Conference, but Duncan is giving him those numbers. It's likely there would be fewer than eight wins for this team if not for the statistics the big man is posting.

Regardless, Duncan's performance has been crucial for a Spurs team with a star shooting guard recovering from back spasms and an All-Star point guard struggling to score. Throw the injuries to Kawhi Leonard and Stephen Jackson on top of it all, and the necessity for a high level of play isn't diminishing in the near future.

As the Spurs enter a six-game road trip short-handed and in a little bit of a lull, asking more of Duncan doesn't seem fair.

But if we know anything about the man, it's that he'll go ahead and ask it of himself, even if it seems there's not much more he can do. Then again, at what point are we no longer surprised? ★

This article was adapted from a piece on Pounding the Rock (copyright 2012), with permission from SB Nation/Vox Media, Inc.

Over the years, Duncan consistently adjusted his playing style to best suit the needs of the Spurs.

RESURGENCE

Duncan Putting Up Historic Season at 36

By Jesus Gomez | January 17, 2013

A couple of years ago, it seemed Tim Duncan was seriously slowing down. In 2010/11 he put up career low numbers in points and rebounds per game, PER and Win Shares per 48 minutes. Duncan was still a per minute beast but was showing signs of decline on offense and especially on defense. The Spurs suffered two disappointing playoff series losses (against the Suns in 2009-10 and the Grizzlies in 2010-11) in which Duncan was targeted by Steve Nash on pick and rolls, and couldn't cool down Zach Randolph or battle Marc Gasol in the post.

The following year, Duncan bounced back and put up better scoring numbers in the lockout shortened season, but his transformation into a jump shooter was complete and his days of domination seemed over. This was evident in the 2012 playoffs, his worst ever, in which he was easily contained by the Thunder defense. On the other end, Duncan was still great, but his diminished speed allowed OKC to score at will via unguarded mid-range jumpers. He was still the best big on the floor but the gap between him and someone like Serge Ibaka seemed reduced. People noticed and Duncan was not considered elite anymore.

Then we come to this season. At age 36 Duncan is putting up per game numbers that only one other guy his age has ever matched, with the caveat that Hakeem Olajuwon did it in just 50 games in a lockout shortened season while playing almost six more minutes a game. Duncan's per 36 minutes numbers of 20.5 points, 11.5 rebounds, 3.3 assists, and 3.2 blocks are unprecedented for a 36-year old. Only Kareem Abdul-Jabbar and Olajuwon have put up similar numbers after turning 30.

Those figures don't only stand out when placed against former players. As this season approaches the halfway point, only

In a match-up of all-time greats, Tim Duncan shoots over Minnesota Timberwolves forward Kevin Garnett in 2006.

Duncan has per game numbers that exceed 17 points, nine rebounds, two assists and two blocks. His defensive rebounding is elite, he's second in total blocked shots, and he has the best individual defensive rating in the league, according to Basketball-Reference. His defensive RAPM ranks him third in the league below only Kevin Garnett and defensive specialist Omer Asik. On offense, he's still hitting the mid-range jumper at a high rate (42.8 percent) while also maintaining his efficiency at the rim (66.2 percent) and finding the balance between the two spots. He and Tony Parker are one of the most devastating pick-and-pop combos in the league, and Duncan can still punish defenders in the post.

He's doing all of that on a team that has the third-best record in the league and the third-best defense, according to the defensive rating metric. There are very, very few big men in the league right now with as complete a game, on both sides of the ball, and Duncan is the biggest reason for the Spurs' success. After two good, but not dominant, seasons, Duncan is having a monster year, and there's a very, very strong case to be made that at age 36, he is the best big man in the league right now.

So why wasn't I more aware of the fact that Duncan was having such a historic season?

I started writing this piece to see if I was missing something about Duncan's dominant play that would make it less impressive or less worthy of coverage—after all, no one seems to have taken notice yet. Maybe Duncan had a glaring weakness that made

Even as he aged, Duncan remained one of the most talented and productive two-way big men in the NBA.

his seemingly impressive play fool's gold. I'm not the most impartial of observers, but I couldn't find any. Ironically, it's all the fault of the Spurs and Duncan.

The steadiness of the Spurs makes it seem like the type of ridiculous year Duncan is having is a byproduct of the system. The team concept is pushed so hard by everyone within the San Antonio organization that it's

Tim Duncan shoots against Oklahoma City Thunder center Kendrick Perkins during the 2014 playoffs.

almost as though if Duncan weren't carrying the team, someone else would; which serves to make his performance almost unnecessary.

Of course that's ridiculous when you consider that what the man is doing is virtually unprecedented. But you wouldn't know it if you only listened to Pop, his teammates, or even Duncan himself. There's also the fact that we've been told repeatedly that these regular season wins don't matter; it's all about the playoffs. The post-season success Duncan and the team have enjoyed makes anything that happens beforehand seem bland in comparison, even if it unexpectedly includes perhaps the best performance ever by a big man over 35.

As I mentioned, it's not only the team, but Duncan himself who aims for as low a profile as possible. Early on, he chose to deflect the spotlight and point it towards the team. He has never given the media any reason—personal drama, real or imagined character issues, tangles with other players, teammates or coaches—to fill pages with.

Every story about Duncan is a story about the Spurs because Duncan decided early in his career that's how things were going to be. Most of the league's stars have had evolving narratives but Duncan has stayed the same: a ridiculously talented, team-oriented guy, who avoided controversy whenever possible and was successful every step of the way. No redemption arcs, no villainy (no matter what Suns fans might say), no barking at people, no off-court problems, no tossing of teammates under the bus. Compare that to

Kobe's tumultuous career and personal life or Kevin Garnett's descent into boorishness. Can you blame the media for running with those stories about older players and their legacies instead of reporting once again about Duncan just being really, really good at basketball?

That's the double-edged sword of the Spurs' boring-by-design, no drama, team-oriented approach: we don't usually have to worry about off-court stuff or indefensible on-court demeanor, but it might also result in us missing out on enjoying Tim Duncan's masterpiece. Duncan won't point out how great a season he's having, and neither will the Spurs. It would go against the philosophy that allows the organization to ask everyone who joins it to "get over themselves." It's all about the team, not individual accolades. It's about the end result, not individual statistics.

I love all of that about the Spurs. But sometimes I wish they were just a little bit like other teams and spent some time to make everyone aware of the greatness going on, because what Duncan is doing is nothing short of incredible.

Other than historic, transcendent, and once-in-a-lifetime, the words I would use to describe the season Duncan is having would be "overlooked" and "underrated." Not coincidentally, those same words could describe the entire career of the greatest power forward of all time. And I think he might be OK with that. ★

This article was adapted from a piece on Pounding the Rock (copyright 2013), with permission from SB Nation/Vox Media, Inc.

For the entirety of his career, Duncan squared off against Kobe Bryant in the Western Conference. Both players retired following the 2016 season.

AN OPEN LETTER TO TIM DUNCAN

Reflections following the Game 7 Loss to the Heat

By Wes Thorne | June 24, 2013

Dear Tim Duncan,

Imagine an alternate universe in which you signed with the Magic back in 2000. You used to conserve your efforts on offense with brilliant but fundamental moves that maximized your potential on defense. Well no more of that! When you aired your decision to move to Orlando by eating an orange in front of Bryant Gumbel on live TV, Grant Hill set his AOL IM status to "Dunk City, baby".

You were now slamming so flamboyantly that defense was a mere afterthought. And this made the Magic's defense laughable, but who cares? Dunks and highlight reels bring in dollars and the money came pouring in. In 2001 Nike made a poster the size of a building across from the Magic's Amway Arena. It was a picture of you with your arms in the air as if you were Orlando's personal savior.

Then came Dunkin Donuts. You were an obvious fit for them. The "Tim Dunkin" commercial aired during Super Bowl XXXVI, and was a massive smash. It had you slamming donuts into giant hoop-shaped cups of coffee. Everywhere across America kids were taking donuts and mimicking your trademark spin dunk into a glass of milk, splashing dairy product everywhere and enraging millions of parents...

Alright, I have to stop there. It is just too preposterous to imagine this universe

Tim Duncan rises above Dwyane Wade in Game 4 of the 2013 NBA Finals.

any longer. See, you are great. And the greats in sports are always involved in two simultaneous struggles. The first is against their opponent on the field, and the second is against an adversary off the field. For heroes like Jesse Owens, Jackie Robinson, and Bill Russell, that enemy was ignorance. With each sprint, each home run, and each championship, they made the ignorant uncomfortable and furthered the fight

Portrait by Michal Dye.

against institutional racism. Legends like Muhammad Ali fought the world.

Then there are the lesser known heroes like the athletes at the Special Olympics. The mere fact they are expressing joy on national television is a slap in the face against the prejudiced. The enemy of today's professional sports is at times obvious and subversive. It is the monetization and over-dramatization of athletics. Some athletes' actions exacerbate this infection, while others fight against it.

You, Tim, are the embodiment of the latter, while LeBron James is a living, breathing Nike commercial.

With each Heat victory the swoosh's bottom line improves. But each time you and your team advance in the playoffs someone in Beaverton screams. They've tried to "sell you", and you went through the motions. But much like when you dunk, you didn't seem all that interested. It's like you're saying, "Buy this stuff if you want to, but I don't really care because I've got to get back on defense." So whether it is by design or accident, you make basketball a less noisy and more beautiful sport.

Your lack of drama isn't just unique, it's inspiring. Your philosophy seems to be "Just shut up and play the game." This can be applied to any occupation. In the workplace, it is infinitely better to not let emotions surface and just do your job the best you can. The best revenge against a rigged system is success, and you have been swimming in success in a system designed for people very different from you.

There are all sorts of dizzying statistics that point to your consistent magnificence.

But the most impressive statistic is: 1. The number of teams you have unwaveringly played for. Prior to getting swept by you and the Spurs, Nike rolled out a new slogan for LeBron James: "We are Witnesses." Well I think I speak for all Spurs fans when I say, "We are Fortunate." We are fortunate to have seen you play basketball.

The saddest part about this season was not Game 6, or that the Spurs lost the championship the next game. It was your press conference after Game 7. You are someone who rarely shows emotion, and there you were in front of a million viewers visibly disappointed. It affected Spurs fans more than any loss could have. There was our beloved Timmy, utterly dismayed.

There have been some uncomfortable press conferences in Spurs history, but this one was the hardest to watch. This was torture. You were despondent, and that hurt. I am writing this letter to say that it doesn't matter what happens next year. It doesn't matter if you retire. It doesn't matter if you and the Spurs are swept in the first round. It doesn't matter if the Spurs don't make the playoffs. It doesn't matter if the Spurs win it all. You have given so much to the team, so much to the game, that it would be downright selfish to ask you to do any more. We just want you to do what makes you happy. We just want to see you smile again.

With unwavering respect,
Wes Thorne ★

This article was adapted from a piece on Pounding the Rock (copyright 2013), with permission from SB Nation/Vox Media, Inc.

BETTER THAN YOU THINK

Late in Career, Duncan Continues to Amaze

By Chris Itz | March 5, 2014

Someone recently commented that Tim Duncan was arguably a top five big man. Forget about his place in history for a minute; he's still the best two-way big in the league. Since Dec 1st he's averaging 16.8 points, 11.2 rebounds, and two blocks per game. You know how many guys are putting up those numbers this season? Zero. He's doing it in just 30 minutes a night, shooting 51 percent from the floor, and he'll be 38 in seven weeks. We've been mentioning it all season, but what he's doing is wholly unprecedented and still underrated.

Tim's been one of the best rebounders in the game through five presidential terms. Think about just how long he's been elite. He was grabbing all of the boards before people who are now driving were born, back when the mail was delivered physically and we used phone lines to connect to the internet. We all know he's one of the all-time great rebounders, but did you know that Big Fun is rebounding at a career-high rate?

That's just effort and cunning. We always talk about Tim's vast array of fundamental post-moves, or his banker, or his basketball IQ. We point to these and talk about how his game is built to age well and doesn't rely on much athleticism, and that's true enough, but it's just as much his work ethic that has allowed him to defy time.

He's the first one in the gym, and he reportedly lives on a diet of blueberries. He's improved his free-throw shooting as he's aged, and he primarily practices the shots

Even as younger superstars like LeBron James took over the NBA, Tim Duncan remained a force in the league.

he knows he's going to get in a game. He is somehow rebounding and blocking shots above his career per-minute rate.

He's been the best and most consistent player for his team all season, and he can still be the go-to guy on offense for stretches. Through all of the team's injuries, Tim was at his best when his team needed him the most. Remember that double-OT thriller against the Wizards in early February?

I do. The Spurs were playing their second game of the Rodeo Road Trip against a hot Washington team who had just beaten OKC and Portland. The Spurs had needed late-game comebacks to win their last two against Sacramento and at New Orleans to break a three-game losing streak. It could easily have been a six-game losing streak but for Timmy stepping up. He had 23 points, 17 rebounds, five assists, and two blocks against Sacramento, followed by 21 points, seven rebounds, and six blocks against New Orleans. The Spurs entered the Wizards game without Manu Ginobili or Kawhi

Always a major threat on the boards, Duncan grabs a rebound in front of Shaquille O'Neal during the 2002 Western Conference Semifinals.

Leonard, and Tony Parker was unavailable to play in the second half with lower back tightness.

Timmy Hall-of-Famered all over Washington, scoring 31 points, grabbing 11 rebounds, dishing five assists, snatching two steals, and blocking three shots. Setting aside the two steals and five assists, no one before Duncan had ever put up 31 points, 11 rebounds, and three blocks at his age. After the game Popovich said it was one of the best wins he's ever been a part of.

Or how about that game in Boston where Manu, Tony, Kawhi, and Splitter were all unavailable? Tim led the team to a road win and put up a 25 and 9 with a game-high plus 18. The Spurs started the fourth quarter up five, and when Timmy checked out with two minutes left they were up 15—the game had been won on the back of Tim's 11 fourth quarter points.

But it goes well beyond the box score. We've always known this. Just like Manu, much of what Tim does isn't quantifiable. Sure there are the tangible stats: screens, outlet passes, and hockey assists, but what about the harder ones? Emotional leadership, sideline coaching, his poise in the face of adversity. When the Spurs were deep into their injury plague and the days were dark, there was Duncan in his quiet way, setting the tone for the team. Unwavering in his determination to steady the ship, to put the team on his back and stay afloat in the standings. How much is that worth?

Tim's one of the greatest teammates of all-time. He's never said a bad word about a fellow Spur. He's always there at the end of games, high-fiving and head-patting the fellas, always the last one off the court.

Duncan shoots over frequent foe and fellow great Dirk Nowitzki in the 2010 playoffs.

When he has the night off, he's the team's biggest cheerleader, constantly cheering and shouting words of encouragement to the guys. When the Spurs clinched the Western Conference last season, the team wasn't so happy about going to the Finals, they were happy because Timmy was. His teammates love him, and he has always made everyone on the court with him better. Just how much is that worth?

People often refer to Tim as a humble guy. I think they have mistaken humility for his reluctance to talk about himself. Perhaps people think he is humble because he will downplay his accomplishments, or that it's his nature to not blow his own horn. Don't kid yourself though, Tim knows he's one of the best basketball players ever. He has just as much pride as any other great. You don't get to be as good as he is without thinking that you're the best player on the floor. Just because he doesn't feel the need to proclaim his greatness doesn't mean that he isn't fully confident in himself.

He's every bit as competitive as Ginobili or Kobe, or anyone you can name. You just have to look deeper to see it. We see Manu get that almost angry look and it's clear that he is a fiery competitor. We hear about Kobe working hard or we see him unable to play, sitting on the bench but obviously caring more than anyone actually playing. Tim's

fire is quiet, hidden from the world, but it's as big as it gets—still burning some now-extinct ultra-dense hardwood.

This year, Tim's played the most minutes on a team that's just a game back from the top spot in the West, despite the team having suffered a slew of injuries. Tony may drive the offense when he's out there, but this is still Tim's team. Just like it's been for the entirety of his career, you can pick a game at random from this season and you've got about a 70 percent chance that Tim was one of the two best players in the game and that the Spurs won it.

We always say that the Spurs are greater than their parts, but maybe it's that as Spurs fans, even we don't properly value just how great Tim is, just how much better he makes the team. I keep asking how much is that worth? I don't know the answer, but there's far more to Tim Duncan than what is in the box score.

The stats will tell you that Tim is still going strong and is still among the elite, but it can't show you what he really means to this team. After 1,446 games and 17 years, he's still the best player on one of the best teams in the league. And he's still the best big man in the game.

I won't speculate on his retirement, because somehow boring, old Duncan never stops surprising. The most consistent player ever consistently leaves me befuddled and amazed. ★

This article was adapted from a piece on Pounding the Rock (copyright 2014), with permission from SB Nation/Vox Media, Inc.

Above: Tim Duncan's steady presence on and off the court was central to the Spurs' dynastic run. Opposite: Tim Duncan beats Bonzi Wells to the board as the Spurs took on the Sacramento Kings in the first round of the 2006 playoffs.

A TRIBUTE TO THE BIG THREE

Duncan, Parker, and Ginobili Each Play a Vital, Unique Role

By Travis Hale | May 23, 2014

The significance of the number should be lost on no one.

Three men, from different corners of the world, became teammates in 2002 in San Antonio, Texas. Twelve years later during the 2014 NBA Playoffs the trio sets a new mark for longevity, continuity and, most importantly, sustained excellence. And in this world of salary caps and taking one's talents to greener beaches, it's hard to imagine the record set by the Spurs Big Three will ever be broken. Which makes that number even more symbolic.

111 playoff victories.

Three ones, three individuals, joining together to create something that will never be duplicated. The three have won three championships together but insist they aren't yet finished, and to this point no one has risen to the challenge to prove them wrong. And while not possible, it's reassuring for Spurs fans to imagine the Big Three, the most successful trio to ever join forces, playing together in perpetuity on the hardwood inside the AT&T Center.

Please forgive Spurs fans for refusing to imagine a world where that scenario isn't possible. Their brilliance. Their creativity. Their leadership. These three qualities have united us as a community for 12 years, and a life without the joy in watching the three is permanently blocked from our minds. Little old ladies paint their jersey numbers on their

With their diversity of skills, Tim Duncan, Tony Parker, and Manu Ginobili formed an unparalleled Spurs core.

houses and on the windows of their Mercury Sables. All year round, young children wear a No. 9 or a No. 20 or a No. 21 jersey and not much else, even in the cold. The three teammates are ingrained in our community, and they are part of us.

And their reach isn't limited to the city of San Antonio. The individual strengths of each has appeal across the globe. Some are enamored with Tim's silent leadership. Some marvel at Tony's flash and glamour mixed with his unending grittiness. And some are drawn to Manu's beautiful stubbornness. His refusal to cede any ground to gravity or the simple laws of physics.

So in thinking about how I would pay respect to these three legends, I first thought of the symbolism in the number 111, and then realized that I could torture myself for weeks attempting to construct the perfect description of each. But doing so is just not possible. Instead, I think it would be more

Duncan and Ginobili were teammates on the Spurs for 14 seasons, from 2002 to 2016.

The trio of Duncan, Parker, and Ginobili led the Spurs to four NBA championships between 2003 and 2014.

fitting to pay tribute to these three Spurs by highlighting some of the words I used to describe each of them throughout this 2013-2014 season.

The Leader: Tim Duncan

Tim Duncan is the greatest power forward to ever play the game, but he's gotten off to a relatively slow start this season. Yet there he is, night in and night out, approaching the game with the enthusiasm of a kid about to start his first little dribbler's game. When the lights go down for pre-game introductions, there's Timmy, sprinting to the basket. He jumps up and hangs on the rim for 10 or 15 seconds in total darkness. Then he runs over and does some hip bumps and waits for his name to be called. In the 90 seconds before tip-off, there he is cradling the ball like it's the Christmas present he always wanted.

While sitting on the bench, he and Pop will sometimes argue. The TV cameras don't pick it up, but I imagine it's Timmy telling his coach to relax a bit. He'll then grab the player that just felt the wrath of Coach Pop (usually it's Jeff Ayres or Danny Green) and give them a few fake punches to the gut and rub their head.

As halftime winds down, he sits beside Pop on the sideline and they both stare at the floor in silence. Monday night, Monty Williams succinctly explained the Spurs in three words. But for this pair, that's three words too many. They sit in silence for a few minutes until Pop pats Tim's leg and they both stand because it's time for Spurs to go back to work.

And when the game is over, whether he scored two points or 30, there's Duncan waiting for all his teammates at the end of the court. He gives them all a backward high five or fist bump as they run past him on their way to the locker room.

And every night for a brief moment, the greatest power forward to ever play the game sheepishly looks around the arena soaking it all in before he puts his head down and walks off the court. And every time I watch that routine, from his pre-game rim hanging, until he disappears into the tunnel, I see a Spur.

The Engine: Tony Parker

And a rested but happy Tony Parker will be key again, even without drama or stress immediately preceding the game. When asked about Parker's performance despite lack of sleep and a bum ankle on Wednesday, Tim Duncan sighed, rolled his eyes and said "He's a drama queen. He's fine. He got plenty of sleep."

But as the laughter waned, he continued, "Coming into the game I told him, this is perfect for you. This is what he does. In situations like this where he doesn't get a lot of sleep, or it's a stressful situation, he always seems to play better. I somewhat expected it from him. He wanted to get that game really badly for his son and the situation, and it was good for us."

Tony Parker is a father, champion, Spur, and future Hall of Famer. And now add to that list of titles, drama queen.

It's a term that conjures images of divas demanding the spotlight and making outlandish demands. Handmade white M&M's in vases of crystal for the dressing room. Homes that are situated so as no structure can ever cast a shadow on any of its walls. Bedrooms filled with rugs made with live puppies to caress the diva's feet, because what could be more joyous than a room full of soft playful puppies to caress your feet?

But in this instance, Spurs fans will take Tony Parker as a drama queen without condition, and hope that he plays in all-out drama queen beast mode for the next eight weeks.

The Heart: Manu Ginobili

Manu is a whirling, living, breathing Euro-step, still itching to break ankles. NFL cornerbacks are in awe of Manu's short memory and his ability to line up and talk trash after metaphorically getting burned on an 80-yard out and up. Manu is the man that makes Pop want to trade him on the spot and then cook him breakfast seconds later.

Manu is the one who hears the jeers, and more importantly, the whispers in Game 4 of the 2013 NBA Finals but stubbornly ignores it all in Game 5, as 19,000 fans chant his name for much of the 2nd half en route to a crucial win. And for all the talk of the heartbreak in Game 6, many overlook the fact that Game 5 was a heart pounding surprise, thanks in large part to the stubborn Argentinian.

Duncan and Parker chat on the Spurs bench during the 2006 Western Conference playoffs.

Manu rose like a Phoenix from the ashes in Game 5, giving Spurs fans across the globe hope. Which only made the loss in Game 6 more painful, and Timmy's slapping the floor in Game 7 more raw. But don't blame Manu for that. His stubborn refusal to allow his legacy to be defined by his failures cleared a path for Spurs fans to experience the highest of highs and the lowest of lows during that six day span in June of 2013. That's who Manu is.

Manu is a brilliant basketball mind with a body that can't always keep up these days, yet he stubbornly trudges on. Hell, even his hairline is under attack from every flank, but he pays no mind. Manu Ginobili is a stubborn frustration, and for that he will arguably always be the most beloved Spur.

So that's it. I could go on for another thousand words lavishing praise on these guys but it's pointless. They go to work everyday in search of greatness, and they do it together. Three teammates, three Spurs, the likes of which we'll never see again. Their record speaks for itself. There's nothing left to write. ★

This article was adapted and excerpted from multiple pieces on Pounding the Rock (copyright 2014), with permission from SB Nation/Vox Media, Inc.

Above: Ginobili, Richard Jefferson, Duncan, and Parker watch the action from the bench in 2011. Opposite: Duncan and Ginobili were opponents when Team USA took on Argentina in the 2004 Athens Olympics.

PAYBACK!

Spurs' Brilliance Leads to Fantastic Fifth Championship

By Stephen Shepperd | June 16, 2014

In what will undoubtedly be one of the sweetest victories in franchise history, the San Antonio Spurs defeated the Miami Heat in five games to capture the 2014 NBA Championship.

What began with the heart-breaking conclusion to last season turned into nine months of some of the greatest team basketball the NBA has ever seen. Soon, the 2013-14 Spurs' creative style of play was enough to (almost entirely) overtake the revenge narrative that was slapped onto this year's Finals, in favor of something more beautiful. We were no longer watching San Antonio exact their vengeance on Miami, one year removed from the Game 6 disaster.

Instead, we found ourselves watching the basketball equivalent of Michelangelo paint, Mozart compose, Hemingway write, and Malick direct. What defeated the Heat was not just competitive, vengeful play by San Antonio—it was pure brilliance. It was artistic class that will redefine the standard of what a "team" is able to attain. The Spurs became basketball's Everest, and franchises will forever kill themselves attempting to claw their way high enough to reach the summit.

In Game 5, the Spurs put away the Heat 104-87 in San Antonio while setting an NBA Finals record for shooting 52.8 percent from the field all series long. Kawhi Leonard lead the team with 22 points, with Manu Ginobili and Patty Mills right behind him scoring 19 and 17 points, respectively. LeBron James led the Heat with 31 points, but Dwyane Wade and Chris Bosh were the only other members of the team scoring in double figures.

Flashing five fingers for five championships, Tim Duncan and the Spurs took the NBA title yet again in 2014.

The first quarter started off rocky for the Spurs. Miami jumped to an 8-0 lead in the first 3:30, while San Antonio missed their first six shots from the field. The Heat were quick and aggressive with their rotations on defense, which forced the Spurs to constantly search for open looks. It wasn't until 8:25 left in the first quarter that Tim Duncan got to the free-throw line to score the team's first two points. After a few more easy buckets from the Heat, Kawhi Leonard made his team's first field goal of the night, hitting a three-pointer with just over 7:00 to go in the quarter. At that point, the lead was 13-5 in favor of Miami.

LeBron made sure early on that everyone knew he wasn't going to let San Antonio waltz their way to the championship podium. James was aggressive on both ends of the court, scoring 17 first quarter points (5-of-7 FG) and looked to be on his way to one of those "unstoppable" nights. Some transition buckets from LBJ and a dish to Ray Allen for a three made the score a little worse before it got better, 22-6.

In came Manu Ginobili with some early minutes to help get the scoring going for San Antonio. Ginobili quickly got a bucket and a foul, hit a three, and found Kawhi open for another three to get his team going on a nice little scoring run to close the gap. Patty Mills would follow with a three of his own, capping a 12-0 run, and cutting the deficit to four, 22-18, with just under three minutes to go in the first. Miami would pull away a little more before the first buzzer, and they headed into the second quarter with a lead for the first time in the series, 29-22.

From that point on, San Antonio shifted into "championship mode." On the first possession of the second quarter, Boris Diaw found Kawhi curling off of a screen at the elbow for an alley-oop dunk that finally had Spurs fans saying, "Okay, now I've seen everything." The Spurs proceeded to exploit mismatches against Miami's bench. Duncan went to work in the post against Udonis Haslem, who never stood a chance, and Kawhi hit one jumper after the next. The Heat defense, which had started the game strong, began to lose its edge.

Confetti rains down on the 2014 champion Spurs in front of the home crowd in San Antonio.

The Spurs had cut the lead to one, 35-34, when Kawhi grabbed a rebound and took it down to the other end of the court himself, nailing a spot-up three-pointer and giving San Antonio their first lead with just under five minutes to go in the half. The AT&T Center erupted in a euphoric celebration as if knowing that the lead would not change hands again.

What followed was some of the most inspired, eye-watering basketball by our guys that I can remember seeing. The Spurs went on a 14-0 run which was capped off by an emphatic Manu Ginobili dunk over Bosh and Allen in traffic, pushing the Good Guys' lead to 42-35. The half would end with San Antonio up 47-40, outscoring the Heat 25-11 in the second quarter alone.

After a slow start to the half by both teams, the Spurs began yet another scoring run, this time with the help of Patty Mills. They kicked the quarter off by outscoring Miami, 9-2, before Tiago Splitter's authoritative block on Wade's dunk attempt sparked back-to-back-to-back three-pointers for the Spurs. Mills and Ginobili pushed the lead to 14 with just over five minutes to go, giving San Antonio the separation they would maintain for the rest of the game. They ended the quarter with a 77-58 lead and the title was all but theirs.

The fourth quarter was as close to a victory lap as you'll see in a best-of-seven series. The lead hovered around 16 points the entire 12 minutes, with Tony Parker (1-for-11 through the first three quarters) finally coming alive to keep it that way. The team's only All-Star scored the final 14 points of the fourth quarter, leaving his own vital mark on the game before coming out in the final minutes.

Nothing was more moving than watching Tony, Timmy, and Manu get subbed out of Game 5 as the crowd showered them with praise. One by one, the future Hall of Famers left the floor, getting love from every teammate on the bench before finally, emphatically embracing each other. The winningest Big Three in NBA playoff history added one more victory to the record books, but nothing seemed more special to them than to spend that moment together. They've done something no three humans have ever done in history, and they looked as if they wouldn't have chosen anybody else to do it with.

After the final horn had sounded, the Spurs made their way to the podium to accept the Larry O'Brien Trophy, each foreign player donning their home country's flag. When Kawhi's name was announced as the NBA Finals MVP, every player on the team knew it was going to the right guy. The soft-spoken 22-year-old, all smiles, accepted the award and put together more full sentences than I think we deserve.

This was an amazing season, capped off with beautiful team play in the Finals that can never be replicated.

Thank you, Spurs. ★

This article was adapted from a piece on Pounding the Rock (copyright 2014), with permission from SB Nation/Vox Media, Inc.

President Barack Obama shakes hands with Tim Duncan as the Spurs were honored at the White House as 2014 NBA champions.

REVEALING THE MYSTERIES

Much More to Duncan than Meets the Eye

By Michael Erler | June 15, 2014

While viewing Tim Duncan from afar all these years, I've found him to be a fascinating character, multifaceted and complex, emotional and calculated. But I still encounter people who believe that there's no depth to him; that the reason he's viewed as stoic and robotic is that there really isn't much beneath the surface. I feel compelled to challenge those misconceptions.

The fact is that as loathe as Duncan is to share his thoughts and feelings with the outside world, there have been dozens of instances over the years when his mask slips, if only for a moment, and he reveals a part of himself. It's all a question of what the cameras happen to catch on a given night and whether we're paying attention.

Mostly, when Duncan gives us a nibble, it truly is accidental—a fortuitous break borne of spontaneous emotion or something he does on the bench when he doesn't think the cameras are on him. But other times, Duncan sends out random signals to the world, maybe for his private amusement or even to gauge reaction.

First, the accidental stuff: the unintentional slips.

It's mind-boggling that so many NBA fans still think of Duncan as unemotional. He's racked up 10 technical fouls this season and 89 for his career, about 5.2 on average per season, leading the Spurs in that category just about every year the completely-insane Stephen Jackson wasn't on the club. Duncan complains vociferously about calls and non-

Tim Duncan attacks the basket over Kevin Garnett and Mark Blount in 2006.

calls more than any Spur and always has. He bugs out his eyes and screams profanities with the best of 'em.

Also, while he's not one to dance a jig and rarely mean-mugs for the camera, Duncan celebrates openly when the moment strikes him, like on his game-tying three in Game 1 of the 2008 playoff series against the Suns, which sent that epic game into double-overtime.

Or when he emphatically pumped his fist after slamming home a gorgeous feed from Boris Diaw, to hammer the nail in Miami's coffin during Game 4. Or the way he gleefully reacted after an "and-1" during the middle of the third quarter of Game 6 last year, when he was having a game for the ages and it really seemed like the Spurs were going to close out the Heat in Miami.

Sadly, the emotional moment Duncan's best known for (outside of getting ejected by Joey Crawford for laughing from the bench) is slapping the floor in utter frustration after missing a game-tying bunny layup late in Game 7 of the Finals last season. Duncan's dejection and inner turmoil was palpable and soul-crushing.

Duncan burns to win as much as anyone who's ever played, but his form of trash-talking, of getting into the heads of his opponents, is to not talk at all. No matter what people say to him, he just glares back, impassively, while continuing to kick butt. The refs may get a taste of his verbal wrath now and again, but his foes don't.

Many of Duncan's adversaries have grown accustomed to his unique method of psychological warfare, but none other than Ron Artest summed it up...

"I remember one time Kevin Garnett was mushing him, and shoving him in the face; and Tim Duncan didn't do anything, he didn't react. He just kicked Kevin Garnett's a--, and won the damn championship. You know what I'm sayin'? That's gangsta."

Perhaps the best example of Duncan in action was the way he—and to be fair, the Spurs bigs collectively—so unnerved Dwight Howard last year that Howard got himself thrown out of Game 4 during San Antonio's easy sweep of the Lakers last season.

Duncan responded with the best "You mad, bro?" face ever.

While Duncan's emotional and competitive qualities are evident, he's less known publicly for his quick wit and his pranking of teammates. New Spurs quickly come to learn that the living legend they watched as kids can be as merciless to them off the floor as he is to opponents on it.

To see this side of Duncan requires a bit of digging. He's a guy who invites teammates to paintball tournaments in his backyard but rigs their guns to shoot wide while arming himself with the most advanced and accurate weaponry. A guy who introduced himself to his pro coach in his native St. Croix by having Pop taste a sugary shaved-ice drink he knew tasted disgusting. A guy who pretended to be drowning deep in the ocean while the two of them were out for a get-to-know-each-other swim. A guy who purposefully played up the "Big Shot Bob" nickname to reporters and delighted in

Duncan and Sean Elliott double team Larry Johnson of the New York Knicks during Game 4 of the 1999 NBA Finals.

calling Robert Horry, "Bobby," because he knew Horry hated it.

After vanquishing the Detroit Pistons in Game 7 of the 2005 NBA Finals Duncan deadpanned his way through a soliloquy about Horry, explaining how his good friend had built a career out of barely breaking a sweat from November through April and only showing up when the real games matter. All the while he pretended that he couldn't see Horry, waiting for his turn on the podium, standing just out of camera shot in the doorway. Finally, Horry heard enough and wandered into the picture, leaving Duncan to feign embarrassment and greet him with a, "Oh haaaay, Bob."

Which brings us to the Duncan who routinely slams into his ex-teammate, Spurs color man Sean Elliott, during pregame layup lines. Every so often he throws a towel or a few basketballs at Elliott's head during the broadcast.

Lest you think only Elliott suffers these indignities, that's far from the case. Any former Spur on the broadcast table, regardless of whom they happen to be working for now, is in store for abuse. It doesn't matter if it's Bruce Bowen, Malik Rose, Avery Johnson, Steve Kerr, or Brent Barry. Duncan messes with them all, on or off camera.

What cannot be argued is that Duncan's teammates, both old and new, revere him, from Stephen Jackson to Beno Udrih. A major reason both Tony Parker and Manu Ginobili—dubbed by Duncan as French Boy and Crazy Boy—developed as they did was to win Duncan's respect.

On the other end of the spectrum, Duncan played with his kids during halftime of Game 5 of the 2013 NBA Finals, at a time where you'd think he'd be more focused on the task at hand than anything.

These are things that Duncan just does, year after year, in front of everyone but not really for their consumption. He plays because he loves the game, loves to compete and loves his teammates. Everything else is scenery and noise, an unnecessary burden.

With Duncan it's rarely too emphatic and you have to learn to read between the lines. In Chris Ballard's wonderful profile for SI.com, he explained his philosophy as loquaciously as he ever will.

Duncan thinks for a second, pulls on the sleeve of his silver Spurs sweatshirt. "Why?" he says. "I have no control of that. All I can do is play and try to play well. Winning should be the only thing that matters. I can't manipulate how people see me."

But that's not true at all, he's told.

Never one for trash talking, Tim Duncan simply smiles in the direction of Los Angeles Lakers' big man Dwight Howard during the 2013 Western Conference playoffs.

Robert Horry challenges Duncan in 2002 as a member of the Los Angeles Lakers. Horry would later join Duncan on the Spurs, with the pair winning championships in 2005 and 2007.

He considers this, then frowns. "I mean, I guess I could. I could be more accessible and be the darling for everybody. I could open up my life and get more endorsements and be out there and be a fan favorite. But why would that help?"

He pauses for a moment. "Why should it?"

Parse that carefully and you'll find all you need to know about the man. It's a rejection of the concept of athletes "branding" themselves through wardrobes and social media platforms, and of fans and media who are more drawn to athletes' words and antics than on-court accomplishments.

We're talking about a man who contributed to a published study titled "Aversive Interpersonal Behaviors," back in 1997. Duncan's chapter, which he co-wrote with three other Wake Forest psychology majors, was titled "Blowhards, Snobs, And Narcissists: Interpersonal Reactions To Excessive Egotism."

The man literally wrote his own manual for how to prepare for life in the NBA.

It may be impossible to fully "get" Tim Duncan. His words and actions off the court are just like his game. It looks so basic and fundamental and boring on the surface, but if you watch it night after night after night, like true Spurs nerds do, it's possible to understand he's operating on a whole different plane. ⭐

This article was adapted from a piece on Pounding the Rock (copyright 2014), with permission from SB Nation/Vox Media, Inc.

RECORD SETTERS

The Spurs' Record of Excellence is Astounding

By Chris Itz | June 29, 2014

On Sunday, March 16, 2014 the San Antonio Spurs beat the Utah Jazz and extended their winning streak to 10 straight on their way to 19-in-a-row, which stands as the sixth-longest regular-season-only streak of all time. The most noteworthy part of that victory was that the Spurs won their 50th game of the season that night. In doing so, they extended their existing NBA-record streak of consecutive 50-win seasons to 15.

Think about that. It's a truly remarkable feat. Its three seasons longer than the 1979-1991 Lakers posted, and if not for the lockout-shortened 1999 season, it would probably be 17—which is the entirety of Tim Duncan's legendary career. Here's another bit of trivia about this streak: if 2014 is the final year of the Spurs' record, it will be 2028 before anyone can hope to break their record.

You read that right. Because of the 2012 lockout-shortened season, when only the Spurs and Bulls won 50 games in the 66-game season, the only active streak that is more than two seasons long belongs to the Spurs. With the band at least mostly getting back together for 2015, it would be a huge surprise if the streak doesn't extend to at least 16. This seems like a record that will not be broken for a very long time. If ever.

That they accomplished that feat while not having a single player average 30 minutes a game is perhaps even more remarkable. The depth of the team and the minute-managing prowess that Gregg Popovich has developed over the years is quite an accomplishment. The Spurs became the first team since the ABA/NBA merger to not have a player average at least 30 minutes a game.

Duncan finishes strongly during 2003's Western Conference Finals against the Dallas Mavericks.

Duncan led the team in total minutes played, which is totally mind-boggling. His 2,158 minutes played was 142 more than the second-place Marco Belinelli. Tim broke a couple records during the postseason, but a 37-year-old leading a championship team in minutes played is just silly. I figured that would be a record as well, but Jason Kidd led the 2011 Mavericks in minutes played, and

he was a month older than Timmy when he did it. There's always next year though!

Once the playoffs started, the Spurs began to break all kinds of records.

Against the Oklahoma City Thunder, the trio of Duncan, Tony Parker, and Manu Ginobili notched their 112th playoff win, and in doing so they passed Magic Johnson, Kareem Abdul-Jabbar, and Michael Cooper for the most playoff wins by a trio in NBA history.

During the playoffs, I was firmly of the opinion that the record was great, but ultimately not that important if the trio couldn't up the number to 117, which is the number they reached when they won the Larry O'Brien. With the 'chip in hand, it's much easier to appreciate the number as well as the loyalty, longevity, and greatness that it represents.

If you did any reading after the championship, it's almost certain that you read that the Spurs' total margin of victory in the NBA Finals was the greatest ever. San Antonio beat the Miami Heat by 70 points over the Finals' five games. Seventy points, including an embarrassing combined margin 57 over the last three games! The Spurs put everything together at the right time and this number is a great indicator of just how thoroughly the Spurs beat Miami on their way to the franchise's fifth title.

The Spurs also broke the record for best shooting percentage during the Finals. The good guys shot 52.8 percent from the floor for the entire Finals, and broke the 1991 Chicago Bulls' previous record of 52.7 percent. This stat is a testament to the Spurs' philosophy of good to great, meaning if you

Duncan poses with NBA commissioner David Stern and the Maurice Podoloff Trophy after being voted the NBA's Most Valuable Player for the 2001-2002 season.

have a good shot but someone has a better one, you better pass the dang ball. The Spurs put on a historic offensive performance over their last five games, and their defense wasn't too shabby either.

Tim Duncan also broke several individual records this postseason. He broke Kareem's record of most minutes played in the playoffs all-time. Tim's 8,902 minutes played is 51 more than Kareem played. That's the equivalent of 185 full games, or 2-1/4 seasons. That's a heck of a record, but Tim also passed Magic Johnson for the most all-time playoff double-doubles on the same night, June 12th, that he passed Kareem for most minutes. He tallied his 158th postseason double-double to break the tie with Magic.

Of course Tim isn't done yet, and he should be able to add to both of those records in the spring of 2015, thus widening the gap he has over active players in each category. Kobe Bryant is next up on the active list, followed by Tony Parker. This is one impressive list, and it's not unreasonable to think that Tony could end up in the top five by the time he calls it quits.

Here's a record you probably didn't hear about. I can't guarantee this one, but I looked at Michael Jordan, Kareem, Bill Russell, and Kobe. Tim Duncan has shared a championship roster with 51 different players. Jordan and Kobe played with 36 different guys when they got their rings, Kareem played with 42, and Bill Russell played with 45 over his 11 championships.

Since Timmy has five rings this means that on each championship team he led there were about 10 first-time champions who were fortunate enough to team up with the legend and pick up a ring. Let that soak in. It's absolutely absurd. Sure, Tim played with at least three Hall of Famers along the way, but he also played with Jackie Butler, James White, Mengke Bateer and Gerard King.

A look at where this still-going run has placed our Big Three among the all-time greats:

Points scored in the playoffs NBA/ABA combined:

1. Michael Jordan – 5,987 Points
2. Kareem Abdul-Jabbar – 5,762 Points
3. Kobe Bryant – 5,640 Points
4. Shaquille O'Neal – 5,250 Points
5. **Tim Duncan – 4,988 Points**

All-time playoffs rebound leaders. Duncan stands alone in the modern era:

1. Bill Russell – 4,104 Rebounds
2. Wilt Chamberlain – 3,913 Rebounds
3. **Tim Duncan – 2,732 Rebounds**

This isn't a new record, but Tim Duncan added to it and he is far and away the all-time leader in playoff blocks, with 545. There isn't a single active player that has even half of the blocks that Duncan has. This one seems like it will hold up over time as well.

The Spurs not only won the whole thing this year, but they set some records along the way. On top of that, they're still not done. ★

This article was adapted from a piece on Pounding the Rock (copyright 2014), with permission from SB Nation/Vox Media, Inc.

BIG FUNDAMENTAL

On Display Since a Forgotten Preseason Game in 1997

By D.P. Jones | July 4, 2014

I own several objects which I consider somewhat sacred. A ten year old Cake t-shirt I bought the night I saw my favorite band in St. Petersburg, FL; the collection of license plates I have been amassing since childhood, which includes all fifty U.S. states and four Canadian provinces; my wedding band; a few old yellowing sheets of paper. For a long time, this monochrome program from an October 16th preseason game between the San Antonio Spurs and Washington Wizards in 1997 was not on that list. But it should have been, and for a very particular reason. That night was the first time a certain Wake Forest rookie put on a home white Spurs jersey in an NBA contest.

Basketball-Reference.com lists one of Tim Duncan's nicknames as "Death and Taxes." Whether this is an actual name someone has given him, or a *The Onion*-style tongue in cheek attempt at humor by the otherwise robotic number crunchers at Basketball-Reference, it is not a Duncan pseudonym with which I'm familiar. I can, however, remember when he went by the handle "Merlin." Since this was Duncan's de facto nickname in October 1997, it was somewhat fitting that his first game in front of an Alamodome crowd was against the newly-minted Wizards.

Perusing the rosters within the program, I see a few familiar names on both teams. Some I know and remember well, even though they're long gone from the NBA. Some I had forgotten, like Carl Herrera or God Shammgod. Other names just look weird to me. Instead of Will Sevening, John Andersen is listed as Spurs head trainer.

David Robinson is congratulated by 21-year-old rookie and prized-pupil Tim Duncan in 1997.

Duncan signs autographs during a Team USA practice in Germany. The Americans would go on to surprisingly only capture the bronze medal in the 2004 Athens Olympics.

There's no Chip Engelland on the assistant coach list, though Mike Budenholzer is there, presumably having just completed puberty. Popovich is there, of course, as was R.C. Buford, but back then, they weren't yet the Pop and R.C. we know and love today. As evidence, I look at the number of foreign names on the roster, and observe that every player who suited up in white that October night went to an American college. These were the days when Jay Howard called the game on the radio, the strangely soothing tones of Stan Kelly introduced the starting lineups, and a draft pick from the Virgin Islands seemed downright exotic.

Even the mighty B-R database doesn't have any stats or results from that preseason game. However, the program indicates the Spurs had gone 3-0 in the preseason up to

that point, so it's reasonable to surmise that they handled Chris Webber and Company. Honestly, the result of the game didn't matter. San Antonio had taken what was already a fringe Championship contender and added a legend in the making. Even seeing a 21-year old Duncan, it was miraculous how complete and fluent he already looked. Much as that might be attributable to Merlin's four years of ACC hoops experience, it was evident something more was at work, something entirely intangible yet stronger than anything physical. Even after seventeen years, all I can say is that there's a good reason Tim Duncan's success and longevity aren't really a surprise.

To be sure, Tim's career hasn't been injury-free. He's had to adapt his body and his game against the undefeated force of entropy. Whether it's used in appreciation or as a pejorative, "fundamental" is the most appropriate word to describe the man. Fundamentally, Tim hasn't changed. In the absence of an objective explanation for the consistency, I'm forced to deal in raw statistics. This, too, feels somehow appropriate, given Tim's straightforward approach to the game. Of all the statistics, one stands above the rest:

As of Father's Day, 130 people can claim to have played on the same team as Tim Duncan. Some, like David Robinson, had a tremendous influence on his career. Others, like Shannon Brown, were brought in on ten day contracts to plug holes in the roster during times of injury. His teammates have included Jerome Kersey, who turned 54 last month, and Cory Joseph, who turns 23 next month. During their own careers, Duncan's teammates won championships with Jordan's Bulls, Hakeem's Rockets, and the

Shaq and Kobe Lakers. Others lost title bids with Clyde Drexler's Blazers, Ewing's Knicks, Webber's Kings, Nash's Mavericks and Nash's Suns.

If that's not enough perspective for you, consider this: Tim Duncan won championships with the 11th pick of the 1984 NBA Draft, and the 15th pick of the 2011 NBA Draft. Yep, Kevin Willis, who was a contributing member of the 2003 Title team, was a lottery pick seven years before 2014 Finals MVP Kawhi Leonard was even born.

Many of his teammates have gone on to successful basketball careers after their playing days ended. One former teammate is now a head coach in New Orleans, another just signed a $25 million contract to coach in Golden State, another is General Manager in Atlanta, one is an analyst for ESPN and another for NBA TV, while two former teammates are currently assistant coaches in San Antonio.

Much is made, about Pop's "Coaching Tree" enriching the benches and front offices of teams all over the league. But how many coaches, executives and analysts gained the invaluable insight into the game that furthered their own post-hard court careers, while playing, practicing and preparing next to Tim Duncan?

Recently, Tim went on "David Letterman" and talked glibly about the Spurs drafting players "whose names I can't pronounce." During the playoffs, stories circulated about how he hadn't talked to Tony Parker when he was a rookie. I feel like I understand that now.

This guy has had, on average, just over seven new teammates every year for 17 years. Some he will always remember, and

some he'll have forgotten just like all the rest of us (Alonzo Gee, anyone?). Tim Duncan, of course, will never be forgotten. Nor, I suspect, will many of his former teammates dismiss their time as a member of one of Duncan's squads.

The old program itself is only a piece of paper with a list of facts on it, and if paper and facts are your basis for analyzing the career of Tim Duncan, and determining that they fall short of this player or that player— that's an approach you're free to take. But what this paper represents is an inflection point, the foundation upon which a franchise reinvented itself.

A fledgling coach built a Hall of Fame career, players both ambitious and accomplished reached heights they'd only dreamed of, and potential was realized. It's a potential which was evident from the moment No. 21 stepped onto the Fiesta-colored floor of the Alamodome back on October 16, 1997. That was only the beginning. ★

This article was adapted from a piece on Pounding the Rock (copyright 2014), with permission from SB Nation/Vox Media, Inc.

THE BOND OF EXCELLENCE

Tim Duncan & Bill Russell Share Many Traits, Chiefly Winning

By Michael Erler | March 16, 2015

On Feb. 26, 1994, while the Spurs were wasting a typically awesome performance from David Robinson (32 points, 11 rebounds, 6 assists) in a 104-96 loss at Portland, something quite atypical was happening on the other side of the country.

In Virginia, where Robinson spent most of his formative years, a 17-year-old Tim Duncan did not make a single field goal in Wake Forest's game against the Virginia Cavaliers. Duncan went on to participate in 1,644 meaningful games, 101 in college, 1,310 in the NBA regular season and 234 more in the playoffs, before playing in another contest in which he didn't make a bucket.

The length of the Bulls bothered Duncan in last week's game. Joakim Noah has always given him a difficult time, and Duncan took only eight shots in the game, almost all of them jumpers. He had precious few touches in the post, which is where his bread has been buttered most of the season.

Still, it's easy to feel that the main reason Duncan didn't force the issue is because the Spurs won comfortably, beating the Bulls 116-105, for their fifth victory in a row. They're on their way to another 50-plus wins this year, which they've accomplished in each of Duncan's previous 17 seasons, with the lone exception of the lockout-shortened 1998-99 season which only had 50 games in the regular season.

Tim Duncan and fellow superstar Kevin Durant talk after Oklahoma City eliminated the Spurs and ended Duncan's career in the 2016 playoffs.

When we think about winning in the NBA, Michael Jordan springs to mind—his record in Finals games is 24-11 to Duncan's 23-11—though if you're of a certain age or at least enough of a historian of the game, you go back to Bill Russell, the Celtics icon who won 11 championships in his 13-year career. Russell is Duncan's spiritual doppelganger, both in temperament and mentality, and somewhat in playing style as well.

In some areas, Duncan is clearly superior. He's more talented offensively than Russell ever was, a better outside shooter and more of a threat inside. Russell, who was 6'9" and 215 pounds, was of average size for a big man in the eight-team NBA when his career started, but by his final season every squad in the expanded 14-team league had centers that were bigger than him.

Where Russell excelled was in his own end, gobbling up scores of rebounds and blocking countless shots—literally countless as the league didn't keep records of blocks back then. To give you an idea of his abilities, in the final collegiate game of his career, on Mar. 24, 1956, Russell had 26 points, 27 rebounds and 20 blocks against Iowa in the championship game, leading the University of San Francisco to their second consecutive NCAA title. In another winner-take-all game, Game 7 of the 1962 Finals against the Lakers, he scored 30 points and grabbed 40 rebounds in an overtime win. Russell played in 10 Game 7s in his career and was a perfect 10-0

Bill Russell presents the NBA Finals MVP award to Kawhi Leonard after the Spurs clinched the 2014 title. Tim Duncan was happy to concede both the spotlight and some playing time as younger stars like Leonard emerged.

in them. Though Duncan never could leap like Russell and isn't quite in his class as a shot-blocker, one trait they had in common was their ability to tap blocks to themselves, or to a teammate to start a fast break, rather than just sending it out of bounds.

As Russell told Bill Simmons in the excellent Mr. Russell's House interview, "I don't [think] they approached shots the way I did. All the guys that followed me approached blocking shots as a defensive maneuver. I approached them as an offensive maneuver."

It's their approach to the game that unifies Russell and Duncan. Both will forever be linked by having played for just one franchise and one coach, though for Russell's final three seasons he succeeded Red Auerbach and was player-coach for the Celtics. There's no question that the two legends had similar relationships with their coaches. A couple of excerpts from

Tim Duncan uses all of his 6'11" height against the Chicago Bulls' Derek Rose in 2010.

an interview Russell granted Michael McClennan:

"I have enormous respect for Red, as you know," Russell says quickly. "It was a special relationship—I actually loved the man. And I never played for him—we worked together. That's the reason for our success.

"I trusted Red explicitly—there was never a single day that I mistrusted him. He was an absolutely brilliant man—his background was in mathematics, and he was a master at psychology. He had the best set of ears that I've ever known when it comes to a man in his position. He would have two or three conversations with a player, and he would know how to relate to the player from then on. He understood that you couldn't treat everyone the same way, because everyone is wired differently, so he tailored his approach to each player. That takes an enormous amount of hard work, but the results speak for themselves."

Popovich and Duncan click like no coach and superstar have since Auerbach and Russell. Their philosophies on the game (no frills, no nonsense, no stats, no need for attention, being just about winning and nothing else) are perfectly aligned. Popovich—and General Manager R.C. Buford, for that matter—are both fond of saying that the Duncan is the keystone of the franchise. Popovich has often joked that as soon as Duncan retires that he'll be "10 steps behind" him, while Buford has quipped, "The truth is we all work for Timmy." To this day, with his offensive role diminished and Kawhi Leonard emerging as the team's best player, Popovich is still adamant that Duncan is the centerpiece, the talisman of the franchise and "the base of everything we do."

Throughout his career, Tim Duncan represented the heart of not only the Spurs lineup, but the entire organization.

Perhaps Duncan's greatest strength is his ability to control his emotions, regardless of circumstance. He graduated with a degree in psychology at Wake Forest and co-wrote a study on "Aversive Interpersonal Behaviors" in his spare time from dominating the ACC. Duncan explained once in a story he wrote for *Sport* that his stone-faced demeanor is a deliberate strategy, a weapon he uses no different than his bank shot (and far more effective in recent years).

"People in college thought I was lackadaisical because I didn't show emotion. They thought I was soft because I didn't yell with every rebound. Emotions must not always be shown. If you show excitement, then you may also show disappointment or frustration. If your opponent picks up on this frustration, you are at a disadvantage. I made sure my opponents didn't know what was going on in my head, I guess that's why the fans never knew either. Basketball is like a chess game, you cannot reveal all that you are thinking or you will be at a sizeable disadvantage to your opponent.

"Basketball to some players is mainly a physical event, to me it is both physical and mental. You must not only conquer your opponents physically, you must also beat them mentally. You must at times outthink them. I have to use my shot fakes and things that will work for me. In order to beat my opponent, I have to make basketball become a thinking man's game."

That echoes Russell's quote about mentally dominating opponents in his book *Russell Rules: 11 Lessons on Leadership From the Twentieth Century's Greatest Winner*.

"My best nights were rarely ones that showed up in the box scores. I was once asked to name the best game I ever played. I thought about a playoff game where I had something like 30 points and 40 rebounds against the Lakers, but then I thought there were so many games where I had fewer rebounds, assists and blocked shots, where I wound up scoring only eight or 10 points, but where I was really far more effective. Those games were always ones where I knew I was in the heads of the players on the other side. I could see how they altered shots or sometimes refused to take them for fear that I was somewhere nearby—even though I wasn't. Sometimes during these games I would be on the bench watching this happen. It was amazing. Opposing players seemed to be looking for me even though I wasn't on the court."

I remember hearing Russell once say that the best he ever played, the closest he ever got to perfection on an NBA court, was a game in which he shot 0-for-8 from the field. So I think it's fitting that Duncan happened to go 0-for-8 on the night he finally got blanked. I strongly doubt he'll ever refer to that night against the Bulls as the best game he ever played, but the important thing is that the Spurs won, as they've done over 70 percent of the time when Duncan's suited up.

It probably won't come as a shock that back on Feb. 26, 1994, the Demon Deacons beat the Cavaliers easily, winning 63-45. You may also recall once Russell told Duncan that he's his all-time favorite player. Could it be any other way? These giants relate to one another as few people can. They may have been born 42 years apart, but they might as well be twins. They're different people with different interests and lives off the floor, but when the ball went in the air their sole objective is to win the game. For those two hours nothing else matters, and certainly not their personal stats.

When Duncan goes without a bucket in a loss, that's when it'll be time to worry. ★

This article was adapted from a piece on Pounding the Rock (copyright 2015), with permission from SB Nation/Vox Media, Inc.

A singular facet of Tim Duncan's game was his mental dominance and control over his emotional displays.

LEAGUE-WIDE DOMINANCE

Spurs Own the Rare Feat of a Winning Record vs. Every NBA Team

By Chris Itz | March 18, 2016

Just over two years ago, on March 14, 2014, the Spurs beat the Lakers 119-85 and took the lead in the all-time regular-season series with Los Angeles for the first time since October 1985. That gave the Spurs a winning record against everyone in the league except for Portland, who had taken the lead in that series (for the first time since March of 2006) earlier in the 2013-14 season on November 2nd, 2013.

During the 2013-14 season the Blazers won the first two games of the four-game season series while the Spurs won the last two, evening the series at 76 apiece. After the Spurs won the championship that summer I spent much time daydreaming about the Spurs winning the first game against the Blazers in the 2014-15 season

and completing the feat of a winning record against all teams.

I had to wait until December for the first matchup of the season, but it was not to be as the Blazers won in convincing fashion, 108-95. The Spurs still had a chance to pass Portland by winning the next two games but that dream didn't last long as four days later the Blazers beat the Spurs in a triple-overtime thriller and took a two-game lead in the all-time series, ensuring that the best the Spurs could do was tie it back up by the end of the season. The Spurs and Blazers split the last two games, putting the Blazers up 79-77 heading into this season.

LaMarcus Aldridge switching sides did the trick for the Silver and Black, as the Spurs completed their three-game sweep of the season series with a dominant second half that led to a comfortable win for San Antonio and put the series at 80-79. And with that the Spurs have done something quite rare: among the four major North American sports, only the Spurs have managed to achieve the feat (the Montreal Canadiens have a winning record versus every NHL team except the Ottawa Senators, and the New York Yankees are tied with the Dodgers and have a losing record against the Phillies).

It was fun, and frustrating at times, following this for the past couple of years but it's one of my favorite pieces of Spurs trivia and accomplishments, right up there with the 50-game winning streak, the Big Three being the winningest trio, Duncan winning the most games as a player with one franchise, and all of Tim's playoff marks. Those all speak volumes to what we've gotten to experience over the years as Spurs fans.

Now if those pesky Lakers would get their act together and make the playoffs, the Spurs could get on their way to owning a winning record versus all teams in the postseason. ★

This article was adapted from a piece on Pounding the Rock (copyright 2016), with permission from SB Nation/Vox Media, Inc.

Tim Duncan drives to the basket over Denver Nuggets center Nenê.

THE PERFECT MATCH

Popovich and Duncan Were Made for Each Other

By Michael Erler | July 14, 2016

Gregg Popovich made himself available to the press to comment on the retirement of Tim Duncan, and the Spurs coach, when asked if he had been able to wrap his head around the reality of Duncan hanging 'em up, quipped, "I'm still trying to wrap my head around on why I'm standing here and he's not."

But then Popovich, a fellow not usually given to hyperbole or false praise, revealed something that was truly unexpected. He said if he could pick one person to have a conversation with over dinner (and because Pop is Pop, the examples he used as the people who would most typically be picked were Mother Teresa, the Dalai Lama, Jesus, William F. Buckley, and Gore Vidal) he said his choice for a dinner companion would be Duncan because "he is the most real, consistent, true person that I have ever met."

It would've been so perfect had Duncan snuck behind Popovich during his monologue, theatrically rolled his eyes, and replied in his trademark deadpan monotone, "Pop, we've done that for 20 years. There are literally a thousand people I would rather eat with than you."

And Pop would be embarrassed and have a big horse laugh and Duncan would keep his face blank, point to the gathered scrum documenting it all, all of us trying not to wet ourselves from the laughter, and continue, "None of y'all, but like, seriously, A LOT of people."

Then he'd finally break character and envelop his mentor and friend in his endlessly long arms, whisper a few private words, and they'd continue with the presser.

That's how it would've happened in my script, but real life rarely works the way we want it to.

The mutual regard of Tim Duncan and Spurs head coach Gregg Popovich was at the core of their collective success.

Popovich and Duncan confer during Game 6 of the 2005 NBA Finals. The Spurs would go on to take the series in seven games.

Popovich has often stated that he owes all of his professional success to Duncan, but he explained that his gratefulness to Tim goes beyond him simply being a transcendent talent. Duncan allowed him to not be a coattail-riding, sycophant coach, catering to his star's every whim. He let Pop coach him hard, treat him no differently than an end-of-the-bench guy, and in giving Popovich that authority, it allowed him to grow not only as a coach in his own right, but it gave him a mandate to have the respect of everyone else on the team, which made them all better collectively.

It was a symbiotic relationship, where Duncan gave Popovich the freedom to coach, which gave Pop the tools to make Duncan and the other players better, which earned Pop even more respect and acclaim, which emboldened him to be more of an open-minded and out-of-the-box thinker, which made the team better and on and on in an endless positively reinforced loop.

Several times Popovich got emotional, almost to the point of tears, during the 15-minute interview, giving long, expansive answers and marveling at Duncan's unselfishness and genuineness as a teammate. The story I always go back to as the ultimate example is a night in Detroit back in 2014. It was a SEGABABA (SEcond GAme of a BAck to BAck) during the annual Rodeo Road Trip, and Duncan was being rested. The Spurs had an injury epidemic at the wing, with Kawhi Leonard, Danny Green, and Manu Ginobili all hurt and had to resort to Cory Joseph starting at two-guard alongside Tony Parker. They signed Shannon Brown, the former Laker, to a 10-day contract just to be a warm body and eat some minutes.

Their relationship has always fascinated me. I think it's safe to say that no coach and star player have ever fit one another as perfectly in terms of personality and temperament as Popovich and Duncan. They were made for another, to the point where wondering if Popovich shaped the team's culture and persona on and off the floor around Duncan's comforts or Duncan adjusted his style to suit Pop's preferences is a chicken-and-egg question. It just doesn't seem possible for either of them to have existed and excelled to the degree that they have in any other way.

It was late in the game and the Spurs were getting blown out. There was a time out and no one would've noticed or cared had Duncan tuned out like most veterans would do in that situation. It was a lost cause in early March against the lowly Pistons, in a practically empty gym. But there was Duncan, pulling Brown aside and patiently explaining a play to him.

Surely both men knew that Brown wasn't long for the roster. He'd be waived as soon as one of the other wings recovered. But Duncan didn't care. He was being the best teammate and leader he could be at that moment, and that moment was all that mattered.

I'm sure there are thousands of those little moments in Duncan's career—things like wrapping an arm around Jeff Ayres after a rough game—and the overwhelming majority of them occurred away from the cameras. He simply wouldn't be as revered the way he is, by as many people around the game as he is, if all the evidence were just the games. He was a comforting security blanket for the whole franchise, a constant presence as the emotional and physical anchor. As long as the Spurs had Tim Duncan, everything was going to be okay.

So it makes perfect sense that Popovich wants him around the team in some capacity,

Duncan and Popovich thrived together, reaching six NBA Finals. Popovich was a three-time NBA Coach of the Year during that time.

however minor, even after Duncan's body has objected to the grind. It makes sense that he still very much wants him in his life. Duncan's always been a stabilizing force, someone who brings an island tranquility and calmness to offset Popovich's "Serbian" tempestuousness.

Acerbic as always, Popovich said that Duncan's demeanor allowed him to "hide in plain sight," as Jason Gay of *The Wall Street Journal* put it. But there's another side to that coin. Duncan was named Most Valuable Player twice, All-NBA First-Team 11 times (including his first nine seasons), and is commonly acknowledged as the best all-around power-forward to ever play and one of the best handful of players ever, regardless of position. No serious basketball writer ranks Kobe Bryant ahead of him on the list of all-time greats. The areas where Duncan perhaps wasn't acknowledged as much for, the intangible things like his leadership, were still avenues hundreds of journalists would love to explore with him, but it takes two to tango and Duncan has never been interested in talking about himself.

We always wanted Duncan to reveal more, not just because of his greatness but because it was obvious to anyone with even a passing curiosity about him that there was so much to him behind the stoic facade. We knew if he ever cared to open up, that he'd be far more interesting and insightful than the typical celebrity.

It was fitting that when Duncan finally agreed to reflect on his career, he did so with a childhood friend rather than a household name. He was so much more at ease talking with Rashidi Clenance than he would be with anyone we'd recognize. He spoke of his competitive nature, telling his pal, "It got to the point where I was with my kids and I had to tell myself to turn it off and let them have this one." He revealed that he didn't watch any of ESPN's day-long tribute to him after he made his retirement announcement but that he "about lost it" when he saw Pop's interview. He confirmed something that I've suspected, saying of this past season, "I started not enjoying myself as much. It wasn't fun as much."

But what struck me the most was his answer to what his immediate plans were.

As much as I would've wanted Duncan to tip-toe into the practice facility and trade one-liners with Pop for our benefit, as much as any of us would've wanted a bounce of the ball to go differently in 2013, or 2006 or 2004, the whole beauty of sports, the reason we keep coming back for more is that no matter what we think is going to happen, we don't truly know. Everything is guesswork and possibility and nothing is promised. It's the time spent in anticipation of the moment, the journey toward it, that makes the payoff so rewarding. And like life, sports are often about disappointment and finality and things not going the way you wanted them to.

"That's the beauty of it," Duncan explained. "I don't have a script. For the first time in 20 years, I don't have a script." ★

This article was adapted from a piece on Pounding the Rock (copyright 2016), with permission from SB Nation/Vox Media, Inc.

Duncan and Popovich are all smiles in the final seconds of their first round playoff series in 2003. Duncan's triple-double in the deciding Game 6 helped to elevate the Spurs over the Phoenix Suns.

WABI-SABI

The Painful Moments of the Duncan Era Added to His Legacy

By Scott Quincy | July 12, 2016

I've been thinking about the one that got away. The painful one. 2013. I have frankly avoided thinking about it for a couple of years now, other than as a hiccup on the way to 2014. But with Duncan's unceremonious press release announcing his retirement, the loss to the Heat in the Finals reared its ugly head again, and I thought what a shame it is that Tim Duncan could so easily have had six rings. He'd be tied with Michael Jordan. He'd be perfect in Finals appearances, like Jordan. It would put him squarely above Kobe Bryant in the conversation about all-time greats. I hate those conversations! And it was so maddeningly close. A free throw in Game 6 would have done it. Maybe Timmy being on the floor on that last play of Game 6 would have been just enough. Timmy laying in that chippy in Game 7 might have done it, too. So close, yet just short of perfection.

But late last night my mind went a different direction after reading so much wonderful stuff from all corners of webdom and fandom about our beloved Timmy. He certainly suffered in that series. Maybe he also remembers it regretfully as the one that got away, but I doubt it, and even if he does, he's not saying. There is a stoicism about the man that I think swallows victory and defeat with equanimity, and that's part of why we admire him. Late last night longtime Pounding the Rock member "transgojobot" posted an image of a rather stoic moment from the great Akira Kurosawa film *The Seven Samurai*.

It is a moment that exemplifies calm perseverance amidst turmoil. I think the

Tim Duncan looks to deny LeBron James in Game 6 of the 2013 NBA Finals. The Miami Heat would go on to take the championship in an excruciatingly close seven game series.

ethos of the samurai captures the stoic persistence of Duncan and Pop, and the culture they have created and nurtured with the Spurs. And that image changed my line of thinking about 2013 and where it fits in my understanding of Tim Duncan, our greatest warrior, now done fighting.

In traditional Japanese culture, there is a principle known as wabi-sabi, the acceptance of transience and imperfection. An artist abiding by the notion of wabi-sabi isn't striving to make a perfect piece of art. Rather, imperfection is highly valued. Life and all of nature are, after all, temporary. Nature lacks perfect symmetry. Wabi-sabi art aims to reflect the beauty and truth of this natural imperfection. It doesn't try to outshine nature, but invites the viewer back into nature, into the real world of rough edges and flaws. And if we are going to turn Timmy into a storybook hero, then it seems to me this is the kind of story he gave us.

He isn't perfect. He doesn't fly above us like a superhero. He's flawed and vulnerable, and human, like all of us. Maybe in his younger days he demolished all competition, but he hasn't been young for a long time. No, instead what will endure about Duncan is his endurance in the face of vulnerability, loss, age, and infirmity. What makes him great is the spirit he demonstrated after his gifts diminished. Endurance and courage among good friends.

Which brings me back to 2013. Never was Tim Duncan more human to us than in

Duncan drives past Miami's Mike Miller on his way to 30 points and 17 rebounds in Game 6 of the 2013 Finals.

the waning moments and aftermath of that Finals series. And for that, I will be forever grateful. He is famously private, but that series broke down much of the barrier that he placed between himself and the rest of us. We all shared in his suffering.

It was so painful we wanted to look away. But I for one can finally say that I am grateful for that series. The dagger three, the missed free throws, the benching, all of it. From the vantage point of a perfect story, 2013 gave us the greatest storybook season ever with the cathartic and joyous year that followed. But beyond that, I can honestly say I am thankful for the loss itself. I am grateful for that series as a thing in itself, not only as a prelude to a dream season. 2013 peeled away the armor and let us grieve with Tim Duncan.

Without that loss, Duncan finishes his career with all of us at arm's length. Without that loss, he's so much more perfect. Without that loss, he is a little bit more our superior. With the loss, he is a little bit more our brother. Without the loss we just admire him. With the loss we can love him. ★

This article was adapted from a piece on Pounding the Rock (copyright 2016), with permission from SB Nation/Vox Media, Inc.

LeBron looks on as Tim Duncan embraces Dwyane Wade. Losing the 2013 championship to the Heat was a rare moment of vulnerability for Duncan, the first and only time his Spurs met defeat in the Finals.

THE LEGEND ENDS

Savoring Duncan's Greatness While Mourning the End of His Career

By Taylor Young | July 13, 2016

"The Old Lion is Dead."

—Archie Roosevelt, after the death of President Theodore Roosevelt

The longer Tim Duncan played for the San Antonio Spurs, the less I was able to comprehend a day in which he wouldn't. As the years went on, this figure that emerged in my childhood seemed to dig himself deeper into my life. Maybe I was more prepared to let go of watching him on the left low-block in 2008 than I am now. His presence rooted itself in the hearts of Spurs fans further and further each year. Now the uprooting is as painful as it could be.

He's been "old" and the Spurs have been "old" forever, probably because his first championship was won with old dudes and his second was won with ancient dudes, therefore he's always seemed "old" by association. Then finally around 2011 he did get old. But, when someone is always referred to as "old" the same way that people say that water is wet or Kobe is evil, it just becomes a fact. I stopped thinking of Tim's age as something that could ever catch up to him. It never did, he was just "old."

Many people like to say things like "When Tim Duncan was drafted, I was 18 and a freshman in college, now I am 37 and have nine kids!" Or "I recorded his first game on VHS, I watched his last game on my telephone." So here's mine:

I'm 26 and married now, and I watched the Spurs win the 1999 title on the night I came back from Cub Scout camp. He won't play next year and typing that feels like I've been chest punched by Kawhi's massive

A lingering knee injury during the 2015-2016 season limited Tim Duncan's productivity in the final stretch of his career.

mits. I won't get to see him give backwards high fives to teammates, cuss into his jersey, or pick unlikely pregame warm-up partners like Beno Udrih, Aron Baynes, or Boban Marjanovic.

When Duncan stretched out his arms after the 2014 title, embracing the beautiful moment and all its glory, that picture seemed never-ending to me. It was like those long arms had encompassed all of the Spurs' related history that had gone before, and would stretch into everything to come.

Maybe that picture won't represent Tim Duncan playing the game of basketball forever, but I can see those arms spread like a timeline, stretching into three decades. Lasting through three presidencies, many NBA dynasties and most of the formative years of my life. He was great at something—truly, outstandingly great—longer than kids live at home with their parents.

I have asked people who've grown up in Colorado whether or not they still love the mountains or even if they notice

Duncan relaxes on the Spurs bench with his daughter, Sydney, and son, Draven, before a preseason game against the Phoenix Suns in 2013.

them anymore. Most people say they don't, they're used to them and no longer say, "Whoa, I live next to a big, beautiful mountain." They drive through them and over them the same way I pass the office buildings on my way to work. I have always tried to not be like that when it comes to this Spurs era, but it's hard.

I don't remember a time when Tim was not the best power forward to ever play. He always has been for me. He could have retired in 2007 and that would have been the case. He wrote a masterpiece trilogy that was universally hailed as golden and then said "You know what? I'm not done." And he kept adding volume after volume, past the point of people thinking he had anything left to add. He was the band with no weak albums, the Steven Spielberg who only made *ET*'s and *Saving Private Ryan*'s, with no *AI*'s. Eventually you get accustomed to being in the midst of that greatness, even if you're trying to appreciate living in the mountains.

The first time I ever heard of Tim Duncan was soon after he was drafted and I went over to a friend's house to play an NBA game on Playstation. I chose the Spurs and I played with Tim Duncan. I watched the Memorial Day Miracle and 1999 Finals, but it was a youthful fandom. I was so innocent that I declared myself a Raptors fan in 2000 and a Sixers fan in 2001. I still knew where my bread was buttered though. The first time I ever got furious at a Spurs game was when they lost Game 4 of the second round series against the Mavericks in 2001.

I truly fell in love with the Spurs in the middle of the 2003 season when my Dad and I really started going to games together. It

Tim Duncan defined the San Antonio Spurs' modern era with his 19 years of integrity, leadership, and unprecedented talent.

just happened to be the season Tim painted his Sistine Chapel. Had his 2003 playoff run happened in the Twitter era, it would have been regarded in the same way that LeBron's 2014 run was. Luckily, since 2003, I have had some form of a season ticket package each year and have been a witness to his legend. Tim Duncan has taught me so much about being a friend, teammate, worker and fighter. But, he's also given me countless memories with my dad and friends.

Five things I will always remember about Tim:

1. I went to the ring ceremony following the 2005 title. At the buzzer, Tim and Robert Horry viciously fought one another for a rebound. It was hilarious and maybe the only time I ever saw him try to pad stats.

2. In 2012, Kawhi's rookie year, Tim took Leonard aside during almost every break in a game against the Mavs and coached him up. It was just a meaningless regular season game in Dallas.

3. The only time I ever remember Tim getting what bordered on criticism from the media was in the 2005 Finals. He was playing on two bad ankles and shot poorly in Game 7, but late in the game made a long corner shot from the baseline. Al Michaels thought it was a three, and it wasn't but it helped seal the third title.

4. His declaration after the 2014 Western Conference Finals. "We've got four more and we'll do it this time." That assurance burned into me and hopefully all Spurs fans. It was like riding a dragon into battle.

5. He always hook-shotted his warm-up gear to trainers when taking the court at the beginning of games. And he used to play one-on-one with Beno Udrih before every home game during warm-ups and shot nothing but threes.

My wife and I went to a Spurs vs. Clippers game this past spring—the Spurs won big—but I was struck with a profound sadness because I could tell Tim wasn't having fun. He was frustrated and I think that's when I knew it was over. His game didn't even really drop off a cliff or fall completely apart like Peyton Manning's or other legends, he just wasn't the same force. His play this year if sustained for a number of years by an average player would have been an incredible career in the NBA. His roar just finally bellowed softer.

Some say David Robinson laid the foundation for Tim. I think David is the most incredible human to ever play basketball and an all-time great, but I think it's more accurate to say that David bought the real estate. Tim laid the foundation, put up the frame, built the house and set the table. He had an amazing crew, from Pop, to Manu and Tony, later Kawhi. The house won't ever feel the same without him in it, but maybe his presence, and the mark he left, will be so undeniably felt there that the house will stand forever.

I hope Kawhi Leonard and LaMarcus Aldridge can add to it, build a second story or put in a pool. But if they can't, it's not a knock against them. Nobody will ever be Tim Duncan. We can only be thankful for having witnessed him and try to emulate what he's taught us.

"The Old Lion is Dead..."

But he lived and was so fierce and awesome. ⭐

This article was adapted from a piece on Pounding the Rock (copyright 2016), with permission from SB Nation/Vox Media, Inc.

David Robinson and Tim Duncan pose in front of the Duomo cathedral in Milan as part of the 1999 McDonald's Championship festivities. As Robinson passed the torch to Duncan, so Duncan has set up younger Spurs players like Kawhi Leonard and LaMarcus Aldridge to succeed for years to come.

A PORTRAIT OF TIM DUNCAN

A One-of-a-Kind Spur For Life

By Michael Erler | November 17, 2014

Some guys talk about how much losing upsets them, how it eats at them, how it makes them lose sleep and drives them to the point of insanity. Duncan just keeps winning.

"It makes last year okay."

Those five words—said to ABC/ESPN sideline reporter Doris Burke after the Spurs finished off the Miami Heat to capture the 2014 title—encompass everything you need to know about Tim Duncan. Though the public at large will never know it or understand it because he's let that side of him slip exactly once during the entirety of his wondrous career, Duncan has always burned to win, every bit as maniacal and sociopathic as Michael Jordan, Kobe Bryant, Tiger Woods, or anyone else that the infernal, endless, economy-driven hype machine celebrates ad infinitum.

You don't play this long, sacrifice this many years, if you don't have a single-minded devotion to winning. You don't drag around one leg for over a decade, playing with the equivalent of a high heel shoe on your left foot, if you're not consumed by it. You don't drop so much weight in one offseason (to the point that if you stood next to your career-long rival Kevin Garnett, a stranger would point to you as "the skinny one,") this late into a career, just to give your knee a fighting chance, if you're not an obsessive.

People don't think of Duncan as pathological the way they do those others because he doesn't feel the need to take all the shots. You don't read or hear stories of fights in practice or different people whispering behind his back about what an insufferable teammate he is. You never, at

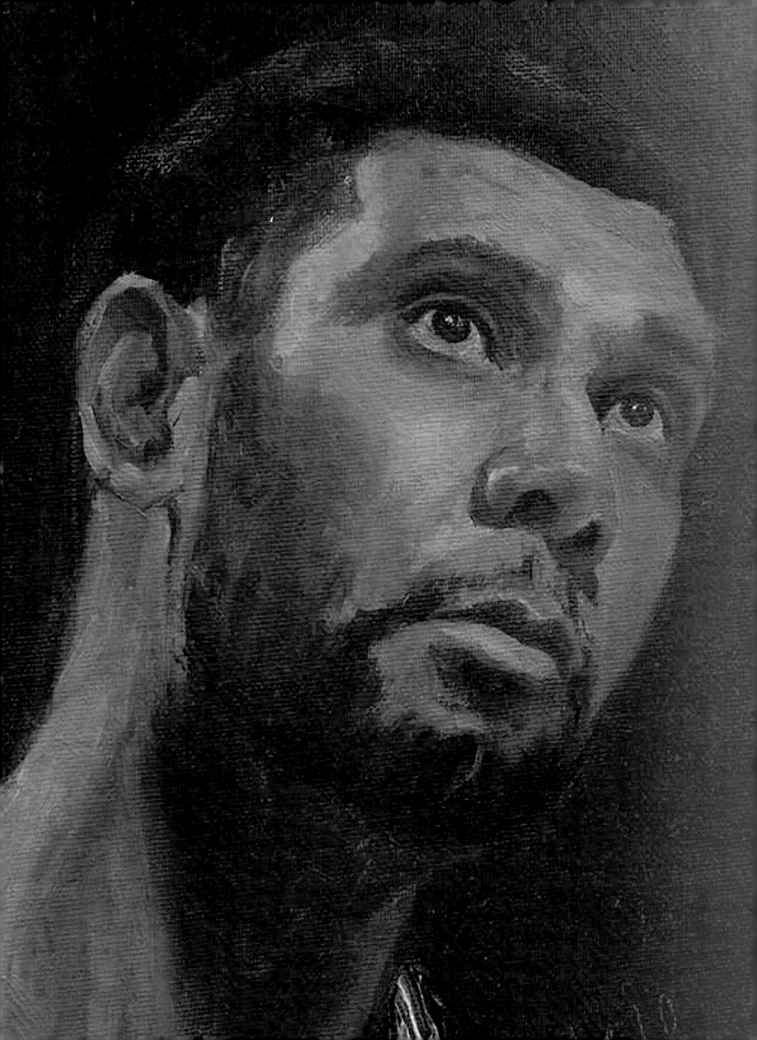

any point, got the sense that he views those he played with as a necessary conduit to his personal glory, a "supporting cast."

In those ways, yes Duncan is different. But when it comes to drive, accountability and pride, he's just as sick as the others. Every bit as sick.

There are great players, perennial All-Stars and Hall-of-Famers, but then, in an exclusive club there are the true immortals of the game, the ones you can't leave out of any conversation. They carry themselves so regally that once they see the finish line of a season, the idea of being a runner-up doesn't cross their minds. You mention names like Michael Jordan, Bill Russell, Kareem Abdul-Jabbar and inevitably phrases like "will to win" or "refuse to lose," get tossed around. I don't even think it's that complicated. I don't believe conscious thought even comes into play. My hunch is that it's more along the lines that for a select few individuals, the statistical likelihood of finishing second best doesn't ever enter their minds. It's not that they can't picture or accept losing, it's just that they can't fathom it.

Jordan was a perfect 6-0 in the Finals, with a cumulative record of 24-11. Duncan, of course, is 5-1, and 23-11 overall. He was seconds—a rebound away—from being undefeated on the ultimate stage, a Finals MVP over the highly-favored LeBron James and the Miami Heat at 37-years old. He had 30 points and 17 rebounds in that fateful Game 6 at Miami, when it looked to all the world that he was giving every last drop in the tank to carry the Spurs home, saving nothing for the swim back of a potential

Game 7. And then, refusing to give in to dejection, despair or "Father Time," he scored 24 more points and gathered 12 more rebounds two nights later.

The one and only time his face and his emotions betrayed him, moments after the shocking realization set in that he had failed after coming so close to reaching the mountaintop, missing a bunny layup over the smaller Shane Battier that could've tied the game with less than a minute to go, Duncan didn't know what to do with his limbs, with his hands, with his brain. He slammed the floor in disgust. He enveloped his head in his enormous hands on the bench. The post-game hugs and handshakes and congratulations went by in a daze. He answered the questions asked of him, looking ashen and grieving. Maybe it means nothing and maybe it means everything, but the look and bearing Manu Ginobili had after Game 6, that haunted, "dead man walking," shoulder-slumped gaze of the defeated, Duncan only had that after it was really over, after Game 7. It seemed to actually take him by surprise that they lost.

Where Duncan chose Russell's path more than contemporaries like Jordan or Bryant is that he never worshiped the false idolatry of the almighty box score. From the very beginning he learned at Wake Forest that as great as he was, he'd need help to win anything of significance. He was raised in the individual sport of swimming and his mother instilled within him a mantra so perfectly in keeping for the modern narcissistic superstar ("Good, better, best/ Never let it rest/Until your good is better/

Tim Duncan takes aim as Los Angeles Lakers defenders Robert Horry and Shaquille O'Neal look on during Game 2 of the 2002 Western Conference Semifinals.

And your better is best") that it reads like something out of a shoe commercial.

Despite that upbringing, once fate intervened in the form of Hurricane Hugo and Duncan took up basketball, the team concept quickly resonated with him. Almost from day one as a Spur he seemed to be thinking exclusively about the big picture, exerting just enough energy and influence to ensure the desired result and rationing fuel for what was to come. Every action was bare bones and minimalist, every leap a calculated risk. He eschewed the highlight play for the simple one and was more than happy when teammates out-shined him statistically in any given game, if for no other reason it gave the media someone else to chase.

Duncan's relationship with fame isn't easy to explain. His lack of mass appeal has little to do with San Antonio being a small market. Few remember now, but David Robinson was once one of the NBA's highest-marketed stars aside from Jordan and his spotlight only faded once he found God and Pop (in whatever ratio you deem comfortable), and Dennis Rodman started stealing his headlines. Similarly, Duncan too started off with a few national endorsements before it changed, as quick and abrupt as a bad bounce off the rim on a June night in Miami.

Early in his career *Sport* magazine asked Duncan to pen his own feature, and the result was so bizarre, so completely different than the usual, wooden, cliché-filled tedium, that it kind of weirded everyone out.

Consider, for example, this paragraph:

"In fact, it's this 'different' nature that will probably fuel my next endeavor, a clothing line bearing a new style for the new millennium. It's called Ultimate Rejects wear. Back at Wake Forest, I had a penchant (and still do to this day) of cutting off the sleeves of all my T-shirts and wearing my shorts backwards. I guess I've always wanted to be an original. One of my former coaches in college, Jerry Wainwright, came up with the name. One day at Wake, we were just messing around, cutting my sleeves off everything when he came up with this brilliant idea. He thought we should start a line of clothes where you don't really know what you're gonna get when you buy it. You know a clothing line with surprise blemishes. You might, for instance, buy a pair of pants, and have one long leg and one short leg. Or you might buy another pair that turned pink after you washed it one time. Perhaps another time, you would notice nothing wrong with your pants until you took them off and discovered it dyed your skin purple."

Marketers had no idea what to do with a superstar like this. In one section he comes across as goofy and in another completely dull. One instant he admits his stoicism is actually a deep-thinking psychological ploy and the next he writes that he's just naturally quiet and analytical. He ends the piece by ridiculing the whole idea of hype, branding, and conformity, making fun of the consumers who'll help him become wealthy beyond imagination. That last paragraph covered similar ground to

Tim Duncan enjoys the 2014 championship parade with his daughter Sydney.

On the court and off, Tim Duncan was a transcendent presence in the NBA during his legendary career.

a chapter he co-wrote in academic journal at Wake Forest titled "Blowhards, Snobs and Narcissists: Interpersonal Reactions to Excessive Egotism." It was a go-to manual for his career to come.

After that story, advertisers treaded carefully with Duncan and he with them. He fiercely protected his privacy. He and Gregg Popovich together built a cocoon in San Antonio. Media obligations were kept at a bare minimum, all of the state secrets were kept in-house and a communal culture started to form, in a state known for a rather famous one. Nothing got out that they didn't want to get out. Duncan was Popovich's top lieutenant, obeying all orders without question and suffering the occasional, none-too-gentle criticism without flinching when his hustle was questioned on an odd January night in Minnesota. It gave the Danny Greens of the world no cause to complain, ever, and over time it's proven to be a far more effective form of leadership to let Pop be the "Bad Cop," than the bullying, overbearing manner with which Jordan and Bryant got their points across with teammates.

In almost any other market and any other situation, the circumstances surrounding Duncan's private life early on in 2013 would've gotten out. In San Antonio he was protected from humiliation and scrutiny. It was made clear that questions couldn't be asked much less answered. He had represented and dutifully followed through in every exacting detail the fully-formed example of what Popovich wanted the Spurs to be, so that when the time came the organization came through and took care of him in his time of need, his secondary family there for him when his

real one was fractured. If his personal situation wasn't difficult enough, he had to endure the hardest defeat of his career. Duncan seemed not just frustrated and upset by the loss but downright embarrassed by it. As if to say, "I'm Tim Duncan. I don't lose in the Finals."

So, a year later, when the Spurs picked themselves up off the mat it should've surprised absolutely no one that it was Duncan who delivered the finishing blow to Oklahoma City in the Western Conference Finals, in the same building where they ended his season in 2012. And it was absolutely no accident when Duncan delivered a matter-of-fact prediction of what was to come in the Finals, telling David Aldridge of Turner Sports, "We've got four more to win and we're going to do it this time."

He played dumb afterward, but Tim Duncan is too smart to sell dumb. There was no way he, Ginobili, or any of these Spurs were going to let one bounce get between them and the trophy again, and the margins of the games were proof of that.

Maybe to casual fans Duncan comes off as robotic, bland, or even the B-word dreaded in San Antonio: Boring. Maybe some think of him decidedly a rung below LeBron, Jordan, or even Kobe. Maybe they think of him as so-so, or just okay.

2013 may be okay now, but Duncan has always been something entirely different from okay.

We're never going to see another one like him. ⭐

This article was adapted from a piece on Pounding the Rock (copyright 2014), with permission from SB Nation/Vox Media, Inc.